A FAMILY OF FASHION

The Messels: Six Generations of Dress

A FAMILY OF FASHION

The Messels: Six Generations of Dress

Amy de la Haye, Lou Taylor and Eleanor Thompson

PHILIP WILSON PUBLISHERS

First published in 2005 by Philip Wilson Publishers, 109 Drysdale Street, The Timber Yard, London N1 6ND
In association with Brighton & Hove Council

Brighton & Hove

On the occasion of the exhibition Fashion and Fancy Dress: The Messel Family Dress Collection, 1865–2005
Held at Brighton Museum, 22 October 2005 – 5 March 2006 and on tour to the Ulster Museum, Belfast,
from 14 April – 29 August 2006

Supported by the Esmée Fairbairn Regional Museums Initiative

Esmée
Fairbairn
FOUNDATION

Distributed throughout the world (excluding North America) by I.B. Tauris & Co. Ltd, 6 Salem Road, London W2 4BU
Distributed in North America by Palgrave Macmillan, a division of St Martin's Press, 175 Fifth Avenue, New York, NY 10010

Exhibition curated by Amy de la Haye, Lou Taylor and Eleanor Thompson, 2005
Catalogue picture research by Caroline Windsor
Catalogue designed by Caroline and Roger Hillier, The Old Chapel Graphic Design
Printed and bound in Italy by Printer Trento

© Essays Amy de la Haye, Elizabeth McCrum, Reena Suleman, Lou Taylor and Eleanor Thompson

ISBN 0 85667 610 1 (hardback edition)
ISBN 0-948723-66-1 (paperback edition)

Cover: Dress by Charles James, 1936 (left); dress by S.A. Brooking, c.1874 (right).
Half-title page: Maud Messel in the morning room of Balcombe House, c.1905.
Frontispiece: Detail of afternoon dress belonging to Anne Armstrong-Jones, c.1929.
Title page: Cecil Beaton portrait of Anne Armstrong-Jones in Charles James Ascot outfit, 1933.

Picture acknowledgements and copyright
The authors and publishers would like to thank the following for permission to reproduce photographs and illustrations:

©Brighton Museum & Art Gallery: Plates 2, 5 , 17, 35, 36, 43, 44, 46, 51, 54, 55, 56, 62, 79, 80, 81; Figs. 5, 23

©Nicholas Sinclair: All colour images of clothing except Plates 17, 46, 79

©Royal Borough of Kensington & Chelsea: Linley Sambourne House: Figs. 1, 2, 3, 7, 8 , 9, 10, 16, 17, 19, 24,30, 31, 39,
44, 46, 49; Plates 9, 10

©Birr Castle Archives: Figs. 29, 34, 35, 36, 37, 38, 40; Plate 1

©The Messel Collection at Nymans Garden, The National Trust: Figs. 6, 11, 12, 13, 14, 15, 18, 20, 21, 25, 26, 28, 33;

Plates 16, 87

©National Trust Photo Library: Plates 29, 89

©Tudor Jenkins: Plates 30, 31, 32, 57, 91

Contents

Foreword

Before the sale of the contents of Nymans in 1994 I had a sad but fascinating task of going through family paraphernalia including the clothes of three generations of women: my aunt Anne, Countess of Rosse, my grandmother Maud Messel and my great-grandmother Marion Sambourne.

Anne, Countess of Rosse's clothes were sent to Birr in Ireland to be catalogued and conserved. Her clothes from Womersley Hall in Yorkshire returned to Nymans on the sale of Womersley last year.

Alas, not many of Maud Messel's garments survived the Nymans fire of 1947 but enough examples were found to give an impression of her liking for smart and clean cut outfits. To soften the effect she nearly always wore a fine Shetland Isle cobweb pattern jersey top with pearls, all fastened at the front with a diamond brooch.

During sorting, a trunk was found of Marion Sambourne's clothes. These had been brought down from 18 Stafford Terrace by Lady Rosse who was frightened that the house might have to be sold on her death and the contents dispersed.

Faced with three generations of clothes I felt something must be done to preserve them. Anne, Countess of Rosse had loaned some items to Brighton Museum, where they were conserved, so it seemed an excellent idea to offer them the remainder for posterity since there were many fine examples of the fashions of many eras.

The Collection highlights many unusual aspects about the Messel women. The family gravitated between four residences, which may account for the sheer amount of clothing extant. Their relationship with clothes can be seen as a reflection of their social standing and of a family trait of hoarding. That the Messel women had the room to store so many clothes is a part of history slipping away from living memory. Their unwillingness to let a useful or lovely creation be discarded may point to a nostalgic link with the past.

Today we are obsessed with essential day-to-day matters and have no room or time for the past and, in our throwaway society, consequently have very little for the next generation to see.

Victoria Messel

Esmée Fairbairn Foundation Regional Museums Initiative

Esmée Fairbairn Foundation is one of the largest independent grantmaking foundations in the UK. We make grants of about £28million a year to organisations to improve quality of life for people and communities in the UK both now and in the future. Arts & Heritage is one of four grantmaking programmes, alongside Education, Environment and Social Change: Enterprise and Independence.

At Esmée Fairbairn we also run several strategic initiatives of our own in areas that we think are important, such as the Regional Museums Initiative, which supports museums in providing appealing and important exhibition programmes across the country. Launched in 2003 and worth £800,000, through the RMI we have so far awarded grants to eight museums to support them to play an enhanced role in the cultural life of their region and to ensure an increased and enthusiastic public.

Alongside Brighton Museum and Art Gallery, seven other museums have been awarded grants under the RMI to date: Whitworth Art Gallery *Walter Sickert: 'drawing is the thing'* A consortium led by Gallery Oldham *Creative Tension: British Art 1900 to 1950* The Holburne Museum of Art in Bath, joint with The Abbot Hall Art Gallery, Kendal *Pictures of Innocence: Portraits of*

Children from Hogarth to Lawrence The York Museums Trust *Celebrating Ceramics* Norwich Castle Museum *Art at the Rockface* Pallant House Gallery, Chichester *Eye Music: Experiments in Abstract Art from Kandinsky to Mondrian* The Royal Albert Memorial Museum & Art Gallery, Exeter, also received a grant under the scheme to research its collections.

We are particularly pleased to be supporting Fashion & Fancy Dress: The Messel Family Dress Collection 1865–2005 because it extends the scope of the RMI scheme by incorporating costume and giving access for the first time to the remarkable collection of clothes which belonged to the Messel-Rosse-Linley-Sambourne family. We hope that the exhibition will delight visitors of all ages in Brighton and also at the Ulster Museum where the show will be seen in 2006.

For further information please visit www.esmeefairbairn.org.uk

Shreela Ghosh
Programme Director – Arts & Heritage
Esmée Fairbairn Foundation

Preface

This book is published to celebrate the opening of the exhibition Fashion & Fancy Dress: The Messel Family Dress Collection 1865–2005, at Brighton Museum & Art Gallery. The exhibition chronicles and interprets the clothes worn by six generations of one remarkable family. Drawn from a unique collection of garments, never before exhibited, it explores how treasured items of clothing, collected and preserved over time, represent family memory and heritage. A singular artistic and creative eye runs through the six generations encompassing English, Irish, French and Chinese style, and a love of fancy dress.

This project would not have been possible without the vision and ambition of the Esmée Fairbairn Foundation Regional Museums Initiative. Their generous support has enabled every stage of the process from the vital research and conservation work to the final presentation of the exhibition at Brighton and the touring of the show to the Ulster Museum, MAGNI (Museums and Galleries of Northern Ireland). We are deeply indebted to their support and encouragement. The exhibition and this publication could not have been realised without the curatorial skills, scholarship, passion and dedication of the joint curators: Amy de la Haye, Senior Research Fellow, London College of Fashion (University of the Arts), Lou Taylor, Professor of Dress and Textiles, University of Brighton, and Eleanor Thompson, Curator of Costume and Textiles for The Royal Pavilion, Libraries and Museums, Brighton & Hove. We thank them.

We would also like to thank the members of the Messel-Rosse families who have supported the project in numerous ways – through the loan of the Messel Dress Collection to Brighton Museum & Art Gallery, in opening up their private family archives and offering us so generously their ideas and memories. We are especially grateful to William Brendan, 7th Earl of Rosse and to Victoria Messel for their encouraging and positive support for this project. We are indebted to all the lenders: Lord Rosse, Lord Snowdon, and the Hon. Martin Parsons; The Royal Borough of Kensington and Chelsea, Linley Sambourne House Museum; The National Trust, Nymans; and the syndics of The Fitzwilliam Museum, Cambridge.

We have been fortunate to receive the support and help of a large number of individuals. For writing for this publication we thank Reena Suleman, Curator of Linley Sambourne House and Elizabeth McCrum, Keeper of Applied Art at the Ulster Museum. For providing additional information and generous support we are most grateful to Shirley Nicholson and to Rebecca Graham, House Manager at Nymans. Caroline Windsor provided vital research for text and images and organisational support. For sharing their specialist expertise, we thank Dr Paul Caffrey from the

National College of Art and Design in Dublin, Verity Wilson, specialist in Chinese Textiles, Susan North (V&A), Lynn Szygenda, (Embroiderers Guild) and Emmanuelle Dirix (Fitzwilliam Museum, Cambridge). Photographer Nicholas Sinclair took most of the colour plates for this book. Beverley Green and Rosa Straw took the appendix images. Claire Browne, Jan Fielding, Jane Hattrick and Teresa Parker helped to dress the mannequins. We are also grateful to Tudor Jenkins for providing images of the Messel flowers. We thank Rebecca Quinton, (now Curator of Costume for the City of Glasgow), for her initial research and documentation of the Messel Family Dress Collection, and Jessica Rutherford, Director of The Royal Pavilion, Head of Libraries and Museums, Brighton & Hove until 2004, who gave vital support to this project and its early development. We also thank the many people who assisted our researches: Tom Cross, Jenny Lister, Oriole Cullen, Philippa Martin, the staff at the Archive of Art and Design (V&A), the Chelsea Local Studies Library, St. Peter's House Library, (University of Brighton) and London College of Fashion Library (University of the Arts), British Pathé, Jennifer Thorp, Whitney Blausen, Desmond Heeley and Helena Mead. We have also benefited from the contributions of undergraduate and post graduate students – Lou Taylor's students past and present – from the University of Brighton. The London College of Fashion and the University of Brighton provided funding support for Amy de la Haye and Lou Taylor. The dedication of a large number of staff from the Royal Pavilion, Libraries and Museums, Brighton & Hove City Council has enabled this project to come to fruition. We would like to thank in particular Stella Beddoe, Keeper of Decorative Art, Janita Bagshawe, Head of Education and Visitor Development and Helen Grundy, Exhibitions Officer. Many thanks are also due to all of the following: Robin Abbott, David Beevers, Janet Brough, Camay Chapman-Cameron, Nicola Coleby, John Cooper, Nigel Cunningham, Martin Ellis, Kevin Faithfull, Roy Flint, Georgina Gilmore, Mary Goody, Alex Hawkey, Su Hepburn, Mike Jones, Derek Lee, Helen Mears, Sarah Posey, Elaine Richmond, and Heather Wood.

Pauline Scott-Garrett
Director of the Royal Pavilion
Assistant Director: Heritage (Libraries & Museums)
Brighton & Hove City Council

Introduction

Amy de la Haye, Lou Taylor and Eleanor Thompson

In 2003 Brighton Museum was awarded generous funding from the Esmée Fairbairn Foundation Regional Museums Initiative, which has enabled us to realise a long-anticipated project to display a rare collection of clothing belonging to six generations of one family.

The Messel Family Dress Collection consists of over 500 items, largely women's wear, most of which was worn and collected by Anne, Countess of Rosse, her mother, Maud Messel and her grandmother, Marion Sambourne. It is a unique collection of exceptionally high-quality, unusual yet fashionable garments, worn by a creative and influential family of collectors over a period of 135 years, from 1870–2005. This is the first time these clothes have been brought together and assessed as one entire collection. We have been able to explore the fashion, decorative arts and style preferences of the women of the Messel family because they carefully kept letters, household bills, inventories, photographs and purchasing records as well as their clothes (Fig. 1).

This book, and its related exhibition, identifies the wearers of these clothes and explains, through the garments, the history, style and aspirations of this family. A close analysis of the garments has guided us to Darmstadt in the 1860s; to Linley Sambourne House in Kensington in the 1880s; to Nymans in West Sussex; to Birr Castle in County Offaly,

Fig. 1 Mary Ann Herapath and Marion Sambourne with Maud and Roy Sambourne and Frances Linley, c.1884.

opposite left Fig. 2 Maud Messel and Anne, Countess of Rosse, Susan Armstrong-Jones, Antony Armstrong-Jones, William, Lord Oxmantown and the Hon. Martin Parsons, 1939.

opposite right Fig. 3 Marion and Edward Linley Sambourne, c.1874.

Ireland; to street markets in Florence in 1898 and finally to China in 1904, 1914, 1935 and in 2004.

The quality of clothes represented here encompasses items that are home made, ready-to-wear and couture. The Messel Dress Collection includes antique Han garments from China and fancy dress of many kinds as well as original examples of late eighteenth-century garments worn as fancy dress. It embraces work by some of the best of couturiers based in London and Dublin, including Lucile, Charles James, Norman Hartnell, Irene Gilbert and the neglected London couturière, Sarah Fullerton Monteith Young, in her hey-day between 1890–1907. The large quantity of surviving clothing has permitted a detailed analysis of the nuances of this one family's taste over a period of nearly 135 years – a fashionably distinctive and romantic style, influenced by historicism, femininity, travel, orientalism and a love of gardens and flowers (Figs. 2 & 3).

The clothes in the Messel Dress Collection are far more than elegant fashion items. They live on as material fragments through which it is possible to trace the biographies of six generations of women from this one exceptional family, which rose, through marriage, from private middle-class comfort to the public stage of the aristocracy. As Anne, Countess of Rosse recognised, the value of these garments, preserved due to her care, lies in their power to hold family memory. As she said, they 'have that meaning of having been worn.'[1] The role of women, such as Lady Rosse, as collectors of clothing and guardians of family memory

FOTOGRAFIA   H.LE LIEURE

lies at the heart of this study and is explored in the first chapter (Fig. 2).

The six generations of clothing in this collection were worn by:

• Mary Ann Herapath (1822–95) – the first generation, the wife of a wealthy London financier.

• Her daughter Marion (1851–1914). She married the *Punch* political cartoonist Linley Sambourne in 1874 and represents the second generation.

• Marion's daughter Maud (1875–1960) represents the third generation. She married into greater wealth in 1898, through her husband, Leonard Messel (1872–1953), descended from a family of successful stockbrokers.

• Anne, Maud's only daughter (1902–1992) became a celebrated society beauty and campaigner for the conservation of Georgian and Victorian architectural heritage. Her brother, Oliver Messel (1904–78), was one of Britain's foremost stage and film set and costume designers in the 1930–60 period. Anne, Countess of Rosse, represents the fourth generation. She married twice, firstly in 1925 to barrister Ronald Armstrong-Jones, by whom she had two children, Susan (born in 1927) and Antony Charles Robert (born in 1930), and secondly to Laurence Michael Harvey, the 6th Earl of Rosse, of Birr Castle Demesne, County Offaly, Ireland, in 1935. They had two sons, William Clere Leonard Brendan Wilmer, Lord Oxmantown (born in 1936 and known now as William Brendan, the 7th Earl of Rosse) and Desmond Oliver Martin Parsons (known as the Hon. Martin Parsons, born 1938.)

• The fifth generation includes Susan, Anne's daughter (1927–86), who married John Eustace Vesey, 6th Viscount de Vesci of AbbeyLeix, County Laois, Ireland, in 1950. She was sister to Antony Armstrong-Jones, Lord Snowdon, the celebrated photographer, who married Princess Margaret in 1960. Alison Hurle Cooke, Lady Rosse, married William Brendan, Lord Rosse in 1966, and also represents our fifth generation. The couple took over responsibility for Birr Castle Demesne in 1979.

• The current sixth generation includes the children of Lord Snowdon, David Armstrong-Jones, Viscount Linley and Lady Sarah Chatto – furniture designer and artist respectively. Lord and Lady Rosse's children are Laurence Patrick, Lord Oxmantown, born in 1969, Lady Alicia Parsons, born in 1971 and the Hon. Michael John Finn Parsons, born in 1981. In 2004, Lord Oxmantown married Anna Lin, in China, and it is her spectacular red Chinese wedding dress, the latest addition to the family collection, which represents the sixth generation of this remarkable family (Plate 1).

In tracking the specific historical settings for these garments, we have been following in the footsteps of Shirley Nicholson, whose three books, based on the family archives and on interviews, have greatly assisted our work. Nicholson published *A Victorian Household* (Barrie & Jenkins) in 1988, *An Edwardian Batchelor* (the Victorian Society) in 1999 and *Nymans, the Story of a Country Garden* (Sutton) in 1992. We are most

Plate 1 Patrick, Lord Oxmantown
and Anna, Lady Oxmantown at their
wedding in China, 2004.

grateful for the careful, informative foundations she has laid down and on
which we have depended so much.

The family's drive to collect, preserve and memorialise their past
remains strong still today. The current generation, including Alison, Lady
Rosse and her daughter-in-law Anna, Lady Oxmantown, have both kept
items related to their weddings and so the Messel Collection continues to
grow, making tangible the memories and lives of generations, past,
present and future.

In 1981, when she deposited the first group of garments at Brighton
Museum, the Countess of Rosse wrote to John Morley, the then Director
of the Royal Pavilion and Museums at Brighton, declaring that she
dreamed of an exhibition of her family clothes on condition that they
were shown with 'elegance and flair' and 'peopled' contextually. We
have tried to honour these expectations.

[1] Letter from Anne, Countess of Rosse to John Morley, 1981. Brighton Museum & Art
Gallery Archives, Coll/9/d/i.

CHAPTER ONE

Messel Family Dress Collection

Collecting, memory and imprints

Amy de la Haye, Lou Taylor and Eleanor Thompson

'Objects hang before the eyes of the imagination, continuously representing ourselves to ourselves and telling the stories of our lives in ways which would be impossible otherwise.'[1] Susan Pearce

The formation of private collections of dress

The motivations for collecting fashionable dress differ radically from other collectable objects, such as the fine and decorative arts. Such garments are primarily purchased or made to wear for specific occasions or purposes, rather than strategically acquired to add to a broader body of similar work. Once worn and out of use, they are sometimes simply kept. If the garments survive, their personal significances creep up gradually on the owner, until, with new eyes, the group of clothes become a collection. Only exceptionally are they professionally gathered. Talbot Hughes and Seymour Lucas, both genre painters, collected in the early twentieth century. Their garments are now in the Victoria and Albert Museum (V&A) and the Museum of London. The vast private collections of Drs C. W. and Phillis Cunnington and Doris Langley Moore, developed through the 1930s–50s periods, are now safely housed in the Gallery of Costume, Platt Hall in Manchester and the Museum of Costume in Bath, but such collections are rare in the extreme.[2]

The intrinsic value of clothes is not, in most cases, financial. Whilst other types of objects are usually collected for their perceived monetary as well as aesthetic values, clothes are kept and treasured for their

Detail of Maud Messel's going-away hat, 1898. *See Plate 3*

symbolic qualities and for the personal memories they hold. As museologist Susan Pearce explains: 'Objects act as reminders and confirmers of our identity … they seem to ease our movement through life and act as medium of passage.'[3] Thus a collection of one person's clothes can reflect, in fabric and stitches, the factual and emotional story of their life, qualities now well understood by collectors and curators. Consequently, there is a movement in fashion curating today which focuses on the display and interpretation of entire wardrobe-based collections, placed in their specific, personal and historical context. A related curatorial interest in the collectors themselves is now also current in museum displays of ethnography, the fine and decorative arts, as well as dress.

In the field of fashion history, the survival of large collections of clothes belonging to one family, or one person, other than royalty, is rare. Four examples will serve here to provide a comparative setting for the Messel Dress Collection – the wardrobe of Queen Maud of Norway, at the National Museum of Decorative Art and Design in Oslo, and those of Heather Firbank and Jill Ritblat, at the V&A, and Mrs Katherine Sophia Farebrother, at Brighton Museum & Art Gallery.

The museum in Oslo holds 200 ensembles worn by Queen Maud of Norway between 1896 and 1938. As was usual with royalty, these clothes were carefully kept in royal archives, as were those, for example of Peter the Great in the Hermitage, and quantities of Queen Victoria's garments at Kensington Palace. The survival of Queen Maud's collection is therefore not altogether unexpected, though the range of elegant clothes, from Paris couture to tailored ski wear, is a fascinating surprise. The collection reveals that fashion was not only central within Queen Maud's life but that also 'she was also acutely aware of its significance as part of her personal narrative'.[4]

In 1921, the wardrobe of Miss Heather Firbank (1888–1954) was packed into trunks and stored away for safe-keeping. After nearly forty years, the clothes emerged and were given to the V&A, all 100 items. Heather was the daughter of the affluent MP Sir Thomas Firbank and sister of the novelist Ronald Firbank. The dates of her surviving clothes, 1900–1920, encompass a narrower time span than those of Queen Maud or Maud Messel. Firbank was a supremely elegant, up-to-date fashionable consumer of London couture, with a preference for 'understated pastel-colour day dresses, immaculate tailored suits and evening gowns'.[5] She favoured the London salons of Redfern, Mascotte and Lucile as well as private dressmakers.

In 1998, the V&A received its largest single donation of dress – some 300 outfits, dating from 1964–98, many of them fully accessorised. These were all owned and worn by Jill Ritblat, who qualified both as a barrister and an art historian. This collection, like those of Queen Maud and Heather Firbank, offers an insight into the sartorial requirements of élite social life, this time during the mid-to-late twentieth century. Ritblat is a modernist, as is evident both in her collection of contemporary art and in her choice of fashionable clothing, which she purchased to wear for specific occasions. She possessed what could be described as a 'professional wardrobe' required for her role as a corporate wife, when dress by Valentino and Versace was deemed appropriate. However, the collection also included work by her preferred, far more radical choice of designers, such as Comme des Garçons and Alexander McQueen. She wore these at arts-related events, keeping her clothes because:

> … at first, as a frugal girl from the North, I thought I might wear them again, or because I loved their design. Then I began to feel affectionate towards them, as towards old friends. Some had certain significance and others – haute couture as well as tat from the King's Road – were obviously special or evocative.[6]

An assessment of her collection shows that Jill Ritblat consciously used her choice of clothes as a tool to navigate and define specific moments and occasions in her life.

Functioning in less exalted social circles was Mrs Katherine Sophia Farebrother, a solicitor's wife and watercolourist, from Salisbury. In 1914, she deliberately packed away her colourful clothes when her husband died and she went into mourning. She never wore the clothes again and the trunks stayed in her house, forgotten, until the late 1970s. At that point the house was cleared and the trunks found, but their history misplaced. Brighton Museum purchased the whole collection because these clothes too, dating from 1900–1914, revealed so clearly the consumption habits of this respectable middle class woman. Less wealthy than Heather Firbank, but also a conventional stylish dresser, Mrs Farebrother travelled up to London, purchasing her grandest dresses from the department store, Dickins & Jones, with one moderately styled aesthetic dress selected from Liberty's. She also patronised H. and J. Nichol and Co. and Jolly's of Bath. This collection, as with all the others, included some dressmaker-made day dresses. Mrs Farebrother's 'Between Maid', Miss E. A. Foan, who first worked for the family in 1903, was able to confirm that some of these were made by a local dressmaker, who was sometimes paid with a leg of mutton.

These four collections of clothes, one worn by Royalty, two by wealthy, elegant woman mixing in London high society and one by a respectable, middle-class fashion consumer, allow us to examine the personal fashion tastes and consumption practices of English women from different social circles. The aim of this book is to probe, in the same way, the stories that the Messel Dress Collection can tell us. This time, astonishingly, the surviving clothes were worn by six generations of women from the same family, rather than by just one woman and across a period of 135 years, 1870–2005.

The survival of the Messel Dress Collection:
hoarders, collectors and curators

MARION SAMBOURNE

The Messel Dress Collection has survived due to the hoarding instincts of the women in the family. Shirley Nicholson has commented that Marion Sambourne, our first hoarder, was the 'family archivist'. Marion's contribution to preserving her family's history throughout the 1870–1914 period was triggered by 'her romantic attachment to the past with its attendant urge to preserve every relic of happy days gone by.' Marion kept all the personal ephemera of her life, from her son's school reports to her daughter's wedding invitation as well as items of her own and her mother's clothes. All her adult years, Marion Sambourne meticulously recorded the detail of her domestic life through diaries and letters, which she wrote and preserved for thirty-three years. Nicholson has commented that Marion was 'just a typical middle class wife wrapped up in her husband and children.'[7]

MAUD MESSEL

The Messel family motto is 'What we have, we hold', and Maud certainly put this into practice, inheriting her mother's deep attachment to the family's past. From 1898 right through to the 1950s, following in her mother's footsteps, Maud also kept 'souvenirs' which held treasured, deeply personal, family memories – photographs, letters and a host of domestic scraps, receipts, invitations to parties, address and note books. When her mother died in 1914, Maud began determinedly to preserve her family heritage. She forbade her brother, Roy, from selling the family home at 18 Stafford Terrace, London and, as Nicholson has commented, 'would not hear of him emptying drawers or throwing things away, and herself dealt with any small alterations and improvements which were absolutely necessary.'[8]

Significantly, this meant that many items of her mother's clothing remained in the house. Maud also kept much of her own clothing. With three family homes at her disposal, two in London and one in West Sussex, she had no shortage of storage space (Fig. 4).

ANNE, COUNTESS OF ROSSE

Nicholson states that Maud's daughter, Anne, absorbed this matrilineal devotion to the family's past. Any sentimental or romantic relic, every family letter, piece of handwork, memorabilia of any kind – no matter how old and faded – was always treasured and preserved.[9] Anne kept simply everything. This foresightedness lead eventually to the setting up of the Sambourne Family Archive, held by the Royal Borough of Kensington and Chelsea, which has proved so essential to this research. Anne fully recognised the wider value of her own, her mother's and grandmother's clothing, turning their hoards into a 'collection' and

Fig. 4 Maud Messel, c.1905.

embracing the responsibilities that this can bring. She was fully aware of the museological and genealogical value of dress. By lending her own, and her family's clothing to museums, by packing away and labelling her collection, Anne ensured that it survived as a precious exemplar of one family's fashions.

It is clear that over the last decade of her life, the Countess of Rosse was also aware, as Pearce has observed, that her collection 'would extend beyond the grave, thus ensuring a prestigious narrative of genealogy.'[10] As Pearce also comments, 'the deliberate dispersal of objects seems to be a helpful part of our preparation for death.'[11] As she aged, Lady Rosse's collection acquired a heightened poignancy and importance to her. In 1981, aged seventy nine, when Brighton Museum's fashion gallery was being put together, she lent a large part of her dress collection to the museum. She wrote to the Director, John Morley, insisting, however, that the collection remain together, as a lasting tribute to her family. 'My prime care is that they should be at Brighton and not passed around. I do feel that they are a … collection. If most of them could be displayed as such.'[12]

Anne, through her collector father, Leonard, grew up in an environment where collecting, collectors and beautiful and rare objects surrounded her constantly. Visits to museums were part of everyday life. 'I looked upon father as this great collector and when we took an interest in the things he loved, like the Japanese allegorical stories on the fans, for instance, he warmed to us tremendously.'[13] Coming from such a background, it is not surprising that Lady Rosse was so acutely aware that surviving dress could trigger the most personal of memories. In an interview of about 1980, in which she discussed her Charles James clothes with Elizabeth Ann Coleman, then Curator of Brooklyn Museum, the Countess of Rosse recalled a telephone call from the couturier, who was also her friend. He asked her about a garment she had purchased from him fifty years earlier:

> Anne, have you still got that black velvet evening coat I made you? I want it at once – for an exhibition – someone will come and collect it. Of course I had, and treasured it as I did all that he ever made me, and treasured too the golden memories that they recalled.[14]

These words indicate that Anne's clothes were acquired for a reason and were very consciously preserved, rather than simply accumulated and hoarded. When she was only in her early twenties, she was already packing away clothing she no longer wore. The earliest surviving item of her dress in the collection is a gold tissue and lace evening dress from about 1924 (Plate 46).

Anne was a passionate preserver, not only of her own and her family's clothing. She also ensured that the family houses, their interiors and gardens were renovated and maintained. Prior to her first marriage in 1925, Anne had already taken on Maud's mantle by ensuring that the late Victorian interior of her grandparents' home in Kensington remained intact and that any new additions were sympathetic. Anne ignored the prevailing trend for modernism in the 1930s, campaigning for the preservation of Georgian architecture. In the 1950s she fought for the conservation of Victorian architecture and interiors (for example, her grandparents' home) at a time when such an idea was deeply unconventional. In 1958 she helped found the Victorian Society, with her influential friends from the world of architecture – John Betjeman, Sir Nikolaus Pevsner and Sir Hugh Casson, amongst others. The society was set up at a soirée held at Stafford Terrace. At various points in her life she was also responsible for furnishing, renovating or preserving Lancaster Gate, Birr Castle, Womersley Hall and Nymans – this she did with consummate skill and professionalism.

WILLIAM BRENDAN, THE 7TH EARL OF ROSSE AND
ALISON, THE COUNTESS ROSSE

In the 1980s, Anne, Lady Rosse, sent boxes of family clothes to Ireland to be cared for by her eldest son and thus an additional group of clothes belongs to the 7th Earl of Rosse, William Brendan and his wife, Alison, Lady Rosse. Stored in Birr Castle, County Offaly, these boxes contain dresses which travel back down the family line to the 1870s. Lady Alison Rosse has added notes and drawings to the boxes giving further, personal significances to these garments (Plate 2). This group also includes key dresses designed for Anne, Countess of Rosse by established Irish designers, from the 1950s. These were shown at the Ulster Museum in 1996, in the exhibition (and book) curated by Elizabeth McCrum, *Fabric and form: Irish fashion since 1950*.[15]

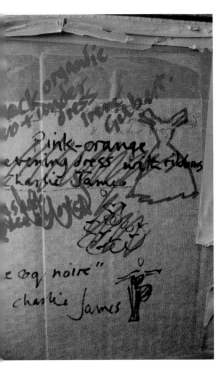

Plate 2 Alison, Countess of Rosse's drawings on dress boxes in storage at Birr Castle.

Museum curators and the Messel Dress Collection

Since the arrival of the first items of this loan collection at Brighton Museum in 1981, this collection has also passed through the guardianship of generations of curators: firstly John Morley and Lou Taylor, then Stella Beddoe (Keeper of Decorative Arts), Shelley Tobin, Emma Young (now O'Connell), Rebecca Quinton and currently Eleanor Thompson. Each curator received fresh items, loaned by Lord Snowdon and Lord Rosse, often with the generous help of Victoria Messel and Linley Sambourne House Museum. The final deposit came in 2005, following the sale of Womersley Hall, the Parsons family home in Yorkshire. Victoria Messel sent the last batch of clothing belonging to her aunt, Anne, Countess of Rosse, loaned with the permission of Anne's youngest son, the Hon. Martin Parsons.

Ten garments were shown in the museum's Fashion Gallery from 1981, but as the layers of clothing arrived at the museum over this period of twenty-five years, each curator recognised one by one the exceptional individuality and precious fashion history that lay within this collection, which became formally known as the Messel Dress Collection in the 1980s. Rebecca Quinton, in particular, documented and began serious research into these garments. In 2005, Lou Taylor's long-held conviction that the collection be published and exhibited was fulfilled.

The clothes and their life-cycle stories

The clothes in the Messel Dress Collection speak to us today about the lives of their wearers, in good times and bad. Anne Rosse's scrapbooks are full of press photographs of her elegant style, confirming her elite social circles and the occasions where she wore many of the surviving garments. Thus we know what she wore to her weddings in 1925 and

1935, to the 1953 Coronation Ball or on the balcony at Buckingham Palace when her son, Antony Armstrong-Jones, married Princess Margaret in 1960 (Appendix 245, 207 & 249). Other clothes in the collection were worn for everyday use and some speak to us, across the generations, of pregnancy, illness and even death. Interestingly, but not surprisingly, there are no photographs of Maud or Anne when they were pregnant. There is, however, a voluminous mauve tea gown of around 1902, probably worn by Maud as a maternity dress whilst she was carrying Anne (Plate 17). A pretty 1927 dress by the Paris fashion house of Irfé also intrigues. It is thought now, because of its date, size and shape, to have been worn by Anne during her first pregnancy. This dress is further discussed in Chapter 5 (Plate 50). Bereavements in the family are reflected in a large group of surviving mourning dress, most of these from 1910–15, covering the period of the death of Linley and then Marion Sambourne. By then, Maud had fashionably eschewed the ugliness of old fashioned mourning crêpe. Her mourning hats are some of the most elegant headwear in the collection. A vast plush felt one, with its brim swept up on one side, is trimmed with gleaming black bird's wings, whilst another, in black velvet, has its flamboyant black ostrich feathers held in place by a large French jet decoration (Appendix 114–20). Finally, still in black, a striped silk, Marshall and Snelgrove suit of c.1914 bears evidence of the painful changes to Marion's body shape during the last stages of the cancer from which she died in that year.

One of the most surprising stories of the Messel Collection, considering the importance Maud placed on her personal heritage, especially souvenirs of her own wedding, was the apparent loss of her wedding dress. Following the death of the Countess of Rosse in 1992, accessories related to this dress, but not, it seemed, the garment itself, were sent to Brighton Museum, along with other boxes of clothes, some labelled in Lady Rosse's handwriting. Maud's petticoat, headdress, shoes and the wedding tie worn by Leonard were included, with a note in Anne's handwriting reading 'my mother's wedding dress and things'. Intriguingly, the dress was not found. It was assumed to be stored at Birr Castle but the dress did not appear during searches there in 2004 and it was feared lost forever.

Discovered, however, amongst hundreds of papers in the Sambourne Family Archive, were tiny clippings from the local press, giving detailed descriptions of the missing wedding dress and its 'antique buckle of diamonds and turquoise'.[16] It then became clear that this was a cream-coloured 'evening' dress, with just such a buckle, deposited in Brighton in 1994 but in a box, wrongly labelled '1908 evening dress'. The somewhat aesthetic styling of the dress, the lack of any wedding photographs and the mis-labelling, accounted for the confusion. A garment can thus even become 'lost' within its own collection (Plate 12).

Gender and collecting

As Pearce has noted, collections have the capacity to take on a male or female identity through the nature of the objects collected, the collecting process and the use of those objects. Studies have shown that men are more likely to acquire 'masculine' objects such as machinery, firearms and those with prestige and high financial value, such as fine art, whereas women have traditionally collected and surrounded themselves with 'feminine' objects carrying personal and domestic connotations, such as souvenirs, jewellery and dress.

The manner in which collections have been acquired has also been defined as divided along gender divides. Pearce again explains that male-collecting activities have often been regarded as visionary and grand in scale, calling for male qualities of competitiveness, reason and ambition. Women, on the other hand, are all too often regarded as consumers rather than collectors, passively acquiring frivolous items.[17]

Leonard and Maud Messel are, on the surface, fine examples of collectors who fall into these stereo typical gender categories. Leonard was admired by many as a 'true collector' – scholarly and serious. His collecting practices, especially in relation to his Herbal books, were meticulously carried out. He also enjoyed the hunting process. In a letter to her father, written on her honeymoon in 1898, Maud described the competitive pleasure Leonard found in chasing his treasures in Florence: 'He beat the men down to less than half what they asked for things. Lennie does the buying … after a lot of arguing we get what we want. Len is perfectly mad … and jumps about like a baby school boy when he gets anything cheap.'[18]

In this context, it is revealing that whilst Leonard has long been recognised as a serious connoisseur and collector, Maud's large, carefully acquired, historical collection of lace, embroideries, antique cushions and woven silks has not, until now, been discussed or even recognised as a 'collection'. Such collections, defined as domestic, are frequently matrilineal and, as Pearce has commented, 'form the female obligation to remember, commemorate and sustain the passing of time'.[19] Victoria Messel, Maud's granddaughter, has spoken about the sense of duty she, too, felt to preserve the Messel Dress Collection following the sale of the contents of Nymans in 1994 and Womersley Hall in 2005. Just like her female antecedents, Victoria has also willingly and purposefully cared for this collection. The official custodians of the Messel Collection are now Anne's sons and their wives, her daughter Susan having predeceased her. They have now taken on the mantle of preserving family memories through their care and affection for these garments. Lord Rosse's wife, Alison, Lady Rosse, has continued the family tradition of adding notes to the clothes and so has added yet more layers of meaning to the Messel Dress Collection.

On closer assessment, however, any simple notions of gendered collecting rapidly falls apart. Leonard, through his passionate collecting of antique fans, seemingly a womanly field, breaks down the clichés, as does his daughter, Anne, through her determining role as protector of three homes and two vast, beautiful, historical gardens, as well as this dress collection. Acting in every way like a 'male' collector, her plans for the Messel Collection were visionary and grand, ensuring the public recognition of her family name.

Imprints and Narrative:
Worn clothing within public and private collections

Every garment in the Messel Dress Collection has been worn, sometimes frequently by the same woman and sometimes down through the generations. However, when worn clothing enters a museum it takes on a second life. What was once intimate, alive and private, enters the public domain and can become impersonalised. As the artist Christian Boltanski explains, 'Somebody has actually chosen them, loved them, but the life in them is now dead.'[20]

Anne Rosse cared passionately about the future use of her collection and engaged in lengthy correspondence about this with museum director John Morley. She was, for example, insistent that her collection be kept together as one precious whole. She was also determined that the constituent parts that comprised an outfit should remain together at all times, whether in storage or exhibited within the gallery. In 1981, Lou Taylor, then costume curator, wanted to display Maud Messel's fashionable 1898 pink honeymoon hat trimmed with lilac (Plate 3) but without its accompanying dress, which had badly deteriorated. The Countess of Rosse, however, insisted that unless the hat and dress were displayed together, the entire outfit had to be returned to her, as indeed it was. It would seem her response was emotive as much as curatorial. The ensemble, in its completeness, evoked loving memories of her mother, and in turn, of her mother's absence.

Perhaps more than any other media, worn clothing offers tangible evidence of lives lived, partly because its very materiality is altered by the wearer. This aspect of surviving clothing – the imprints we leave upon our possessions – has been little explored within museology. A garment's shaping can distort to echo body contours. It can become imbued with personal scent and bear the marks of wear, from fabric erosion at hem, cuffs and neck to stains that are absorbed or linger on the surface of the cloth. For example, the bright pink lipstick traces on Anne's wedding dress for her marriage in 1925 to Ronald Armstrong-Jones were not removed for display purposes for this exhibition, because these have become critical to the integrity and touching, personal history of the garment. Much of the Messel family clothing was homemade or customised, and thus is even more intensely personal.

Fig. 5 Note written by Maud Messel, 1948.

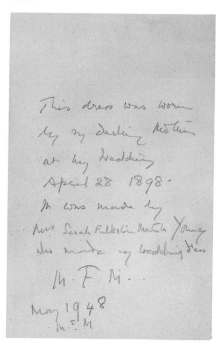

Plate 3 Maud Messel's going-away hat, 1898.

Anne thus determinedly ensured that the specific family meanings attached to her collection remained intact. One of her strategies was to place handwritten notes with some of the garments or to write on the boxes that housed them, like her mother before her. Maud tucked a note into the box containing the dress worn by her mother at her wedding in 1898 (Fig. 5). Anne wrote several notes kept with the clothes housed at Birr Castle. The earliest was placed with her 1925 wedding dress: 'train is kept separately for court use' (Plate 48). A bottle-green, wool-crêpe dress with an ornate beaded neckline, has a note pinned to it which reads: 'Had a wonderful time in this dress am ashamed to say. 1941!!' (see Chapter 7 and Plate 4). That such a dress, with its elaborate decoration, dated to 1941 is intriguing, but it is the handwritten note that really arouses curiosity. We want to learn more about the biography of the garment and its wearer. Where was it worn and what sort of a 'wonderful time' was had wearing it, in the midst of war? Why was it kept, and why did Anne add this note, which hints at so much but tells so little? We know from archival research that Anne's war activities were far from frivolous, as the note might suggest. The dress clearly recalls a happy memory, but beyond that supposition, the story remains a mystery.

Anne, in these ways, added her memories on to her clothes, giving

further layers of meaning to a medium already eloquent in its power to communicate. Indeed, as museologist Gaynor Kavanagh observes, 'transference of emotions and memory on to the concreteness of the object separates that object from the run-of-the-mill and appears to invest it with something almost magical.'[21]

These magical memories were so powerful that Anne even clung on to fragmenting clothes. Some are now far too fragile to be placed on a mannequin, including, sadly, Maud Messel's much loved going-away outfit of 1898, the one she wore with her lilac hat (Plate 5). Fragmenting clothes are nevertheless of value because they possess a beauty and poignancy which can be likened to human vulnerability and indeed, to the characters who once inhabited them. Examining such delicate pieces within collections is an experience savoured by curator, conservator and private collector, but is all too often denied to the museum visitor.

Having made the decision to display some of the more disintegrated Messel garments in this way, it was with great interest that in 1981 we found correspondence between the Countess of Rosse and John Morley, Director of the Royal Pavilion and Museums. This suggests that Anne would have approved these curatorial interventions. She wrote the following insightful and carefully considered statement: 'All period dresses, if they have that meaning of being worn, if only once, become frail. Think what Mary Queen of Scots' be-heading dress would be like – it would have meaning.' She then went on to raise her concern that her damaged silk dresses were never to be repaired with modern synthetic

Plate 4 Jacqmar dress in storage box with note written by Anne, Countess of Rosse, 1941.

Plate 5 Shattered silk lining of Maud Messel's going-away dress, 1898.

materials, adding sensitively, 'Their frailty is in itself their magic, don't you think?'[22]

The Messel Dress Collection demonstrates that the importance of a wardrobe-based dress collection, such as this, lies in its power to carry specific and deeply personal family memories across the passages of time. The survival of these garments highlights the role of the Sambourne-Messel-Rosse women as guardians of the memories and heritage of this famously creative and influential family. In this collection, we have the clothes of six generations. The clothes speak to us today eloquently about their wearers' lives, public and personal representations, their tastes, interests, passions and loving relationships to one another. The challenge we have faced, in writing this book and in displaying the Messel Dress Collection, has been, as the artist Christian Boltanski proposes, to give the garments 'a new life'.[23]

[1] Susan M Pearce, *Museums, Objects and Collections*, Leicester University Press, 1993, p. 47.

[2] Lou Taylor, *Establishing Dress History*, Manchester University Press, Manchester, 2004, Chapter 4.

[3] Susan Pearce, *Museums, Objects and Collections*, p. 55.

[4] Amy de la Haye, 'Fit for a Queen', *V&A Magazine*, Winter, 2003–04, p. 45.

[5] Valerie Mendes, 'Women's Dress since 1900' in N. Rothstein (ed.) *Four Hundred Years of Fashion*, V&A, London, 1984, p. 80.

[6] Amy de la Haye, Sally Brampton and Elizabeth Wilson, *One Woman's Wardrobe*, V&A, London, 1998, p. 14.

[7] Shirley Nicholson, *A Victorian Household*, Barrie Jenkins, 1994, pp. 6–10.

[8] Ibid., p. 216.

[9] Ibid., p. 72.

[10] Susan Pearce, *Collecting in Contemporary Practice*, Sage, London p. 66.

[11] Susan Pearce, *Museums, Objects and Collections,* pp. 59–60.

[12] Letter from the Countess of Rosse to John Morley, 13 April 1981, Brighton Museum Archives.

[13] Charles Castle, *Oliver Messel, A Biography*, Thames and Hudson, London, 1986, p. 25.

[14] Elizabeth Anne Coleman, The Genius of Charles James, Brooklyn Holt, Rinehart, and Winston, 1982, p. 111.

[15] Elizabeth McCrum, *Fabric and Form: Irish fashion since 1950,* Stroud, Sutton, 1996.

[16] *The Pall Mall Gazette*, 28 April 1898, Sambourne Family Archive, ST/7/2/25-33

[17] Susan Pearce, *Museums, Objects and Collections*, pp. 136–38.

[18] Samboure Family Archives, ST/2/2/527.

[19] Susan Pearce, *Collecting in Contemporary Practice*, p. 106.

[20] Christian Boltanski, Didier Semin, Tamar Garb and Donald Kuspit, Phaidon, London, 1997, p. 19.

[21] Gaynor Kavanagh, *Dream Spaces, Memory and the Museum*, Leicester University Press, London, 2000, p. 22.

[22] Letter from the Countess of Rosse to John Morley, April 1981. Brighton Museum archives.

[23] Christian Botanski, p. 19.

CHAPTER TWO

The First & Second Generations

Family history, houses and the evolution of a dress collection

Lou Taylor, Eleanor Thompson and Reena Suleman

The story of this dress collection starts with the garments that survive from its two founding families: the Messels and the Sambournes, who finally came together as one happily extended family upon the marriage of Leonard Messel to Maud Sambourne in 1898. The design of these clothes, dating from 1870 to 1914, mirrors the social and cultural interests of this first and second generation. Our story starts with the Messel family in Germany and the Herapath family in London.

Ludwig and Annie Messel

Ludwig Messel, the father of Leonard Messel, came from a wealthy Jewish banking family from Darmstadt. Shirley Nicholson, in her extensive research on the Messels,[1] writes that his father, Simon Messel, who died in 1859, was financial advisor to the Grand Duke of Hesse and the Tsar of Russia. In 1846 Simon married Emile Lindheim and Ludwig was born a year later. Typically of many Jewish families of their wealth and class, they were thoroughly assimilated into German society. Ludwig's brother Alfred Messel (1853–1909) was a successful architect in Berlin, famous for his progressive, modern style. He designed, for example, no. 39, Am Grossen, Wannsee, in 1900–1902, for the publisher Ferdinand Springer.[2] Messel's most famous work was his celebrated Wertheim Department Store in Berlin of 1904.[3]

Detail of mourning bodice, 1884–85. *See Plate 6*

Finding life financially difficult, Ludwig settled in London in the late 1860s with his brother Rudolf, who became a scientist. Ludwig joined the American stock-broking firm, Seligman Bros, as a clerk. In 1871 he married Annie Cussans. Nicholson writes that the wedding took place in a Nonconformist chapel in Brixton because Ludwig and his siblings had become Christians by the time they reached adulthood. By 1873, Ludwig, 'a man of energy and vision,'[4] had set up his own successful stock-and-share-broking company in the City. Nicholson recounts that in 1874 they moved to Pembridge Villas, Kensington (Fig. 6) when their eldest son Leonard was two years old. They were to have five more children. In 1880 they moved again to the grander area of Westbourne Terrace. Nicholson notes that Ludwig and Annie 'filled their house with beautiful things' and that Ludwig 'had a connoisseur's eye, enjoying music and painting'.[5] He was by then wealthy enough to commission the well-established Jewish artist, Solomon J. Solomon, to paint Annie's portrait in 1885.

Fig. 6 Ludwig and Annie Messel, c.1900.

Nymans

In 1890, Ludwig bought the house and surrounding estate of Nymans, on the Sussex Weald. He enlarged the building, which was originally a small Regency villa. Nicholson has charted the development of this world-famous garden by Ludwig and his head gardener, James Comber, with its Pinetum, established in 1896, and its heath garden with its stone Japanese lanterns purchased from the Japanese Exhibition in London in 1903.[6] The garden is renowned for cross-bred magnolias, established at Nymans by Ludwig Messel by 1905. By 1916, the garden also featured eighty species of rhododendrons.[7]

right Plate 6 Mary Ann Herapath's mourning bodice, c.1884–85.

No clothing belonging to either Ludwig Messel or his wife, Annie, has survived, though the gardens at Nymans remain as their living legacy to the wider world. It is through their eldest son, Leonard, that the direct family line related to this collection passes.

Fig. 7 Mary Ann Herapath, c.1875.

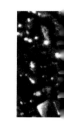

The Herapath family

Of key significance to this complex family history is the fact that Ludwig was a friend of Edward Linley Sambourne, the *Punch* cartoonist, whose wife, Marion, 'was the daughter of Spencer Herapath, a stockbroker, with a scientific background, and an office almost next door to that of L. Messel in the City'.[8] It was this fortuitous relationship that finally led to the marriage of their children.

All of this is reflected in the dress collection. There are two surviving garments – mourning bodices – worn by Spencer Herapath's wife, Mary Ann (Fig. 7). These date from around 1884–85, after the death of Spencer Herapath, and were carefully preserved in memoriam by Mary Ann's daughter, Marion Sambourne. The first bodice is made up in dull black woollen cloth, trimmed with black silk mourning crape and fringes of black glass beads, some in the shape of tiny crosses. This was ordered from Madame Elphick of Bond Street. The combination of crape and beading indicate that this would have been worn in the second stage of a respectable widow's mourning. The second bodice, from Mrs J.J. Carnley, in black silk brocaded in a floral design, is also trimmed with black bead appliqué work (Appendix 2). The lack of crape, however, indicates that this would have been worn during Mary Ann Herapath's final stage of mourning for her husband. Elegantly styled, both bodices adhere to the socially correct complexities of mourning etiquette and indicate Mary Ann's careful sense of well-to-do respectability (Plate 6).

The marriage of Linley Sambourne to Marion Herapath – setting up home

The marriage of Mary Ann's daughter, Marion, to Edward Linley Sambourne took place on 20 October, 1874. This was, aside from the poorer circumstances of the groom, a conventional union of two comfortable middle-class Victorian families (Fig. 3). Nicholson suggests that Marion was something of a 'catch' for Sambourne, whose own father was in trade. Despite this and the nature of his profession, there seems to have been no suggestion that Marion's parents disapproved of the match, and the Sambourne's marriage was a long and generally happy one.

The couple set up home, near to Marion's family, at 18 Stafford Terrace, Kensington and had two children – Maud and Roy. Linley Sambourne's career, as cartoonist for the satirical magazine, *Punch* and the eclectic 'artistic' interiors of 18 Stafford Terrace was, however, by no means conventional. The couple's social circle was also somewhat extraordinary, bringing them into contact with many of the leading figures of late Victorian painting, theatre and literature.

Linley Sambourne's professional contacts were usually the source of their introduction but Marion could count the wives of prominent artists such as Luke Fildes, Marcus Stone, Sir Lawrence Alma-Tadema and Joseph Boehm as close friends. Dinners could be grand affairs, followed by conversation and entertainments with a cab home in the early hours. The local artists 'colony' of Melbury Road comprising Val Prinsep, G.F. Watts, Frederic Leighton, Sir Hamo Thornycroft, in addition to Fildes and Stone, were well known to the Sambournes.

Marion Sambourne's style

Marion Sambourne was, of course, required to dress correctly for all the occasions in her busy life and needed a wardrobe of day, evening, summer, winter, city and country clothes. The Messel Dress Collection contains a cross section of such garments, including a group dating from about 1870 to 1914. Victoria Messel confirms in her preface for this book that these had remained at Marion's home at Stafford Terrace until removed to Nymans by Anne, Lady Rosse for safe keeping, probably in the 1960s.

The earliest Sambourne dress is an unlabelled, purple silk moiré evening bodice and skirt, dating from about 1870 (Appendix 3). The second is a bustle-back dress, dating to about 1874, in pink with a deeper pink stripe (Plate 7). Both an evening bodice and a day jacket survive. The first has a boat-shaped décolletage, short sleeves, centre back lacing and is trimmed with blonde lace and amber-brown silk. One sleeve has become detached from the matching day jacket. The skirt, in matching pink silk, is trained and fashionably ruched, with a corresponding amber panel down the centre back and amber bows on the centre front. The dress is labelled on the waistband, 'S.A. BROOKING, 23, WESTBOURNE GROVE, LONDON.W' and could well be related to Marion Herapath's wedding to Linley Sambourne in 1874. This dress is a key artefact in the history of this dress collection, as will become clear (Plate 8). A dress, also from the same period, is made up in brown ribbed silk, trimmed smartly with white ribbed silk and cut with a fishtail centre back (Appendix 4).

Plate 8 Dressmaker label, c.1874.

right Plate 7 An early Sambourne dress by S.A. Brooking, c.1874.

Dressed in these clothes, Marion would have been conventionally smart, rather than showily elegant, and suitably dressed to support her husband's social position. Whilst to all intents and purposes 'an artist', Sambourne, through his position at the increasingly important *Punch* magazine, had a greater degree of social respectability than might be accorded a general commercial draughtsman (his previous career). In any event, his progress to the role of Chief Cartoonist at Punch made him a well-known figure and a friend of prominent industrialists and men of business. Marion's style in dress exactly reflects all of this. She eschewed even the slightest indication of 'greenery-yallery' aesthetic dress all her life, a style frequently worn in the late nineteenth century by the wives and daughters of many of the artistic families with whom Marion socialised.

Marion seems to have been content with the supporting role of wife and mother. Her diaries record a steady, if occasionally, exasperated, affection for her husband. There is little doubt that Sambourne's work, whilst never of great pecuniary benefit, was together with the children, the focus of family life. Their daughter, Maud, born in 1875, a charming and engaging personality throughout her childhood and youth, evidently inherited her father's artistic sensibilities. By way of contrast, the Sambourne's son, born in 1878 and christened Mawdley (but known as Roy), was a difficult child who rarely justified the investment in time and money expended upon him by his parents, though his sense of fun represented the other side of his father's personality.

Linley Sambourne House and interiors

The Sambourne family home, 18 Stafford Terrace, can be considered a fair reflection of the Sambournes themselves. Outwardly the house is one of an identical terrace of dwellings whose appearance is one of conventional respectability. A great deal is known about this house and about Marion Sambourne's wardrobe, because not only does the house's interior survive intact but so too do thousands of letters, bills, photographs, formal documents and above all Marion Sambourne's dairies, now housed in the Sambourne Family Archive in Kensington Reference Library. In 1988 Shirley Nicholson published her detailed and fascinating book, *A Victorian Household*, from which much of this information has been drawn.[9]

18 Stafford Terrace comprised identical accommodation to that of all the other homes in the street. Each floor consisted of two rooms; a morning room and dining room on the ground floor with a drawing room and front parlour at first floor level being the principal spaces. Toilets and bathrooms were located on each of the half-landings with service accommodation (kitchens, larders etc.) in the basement. Bedrooms were at the top of the house with servants' rooms occupying the attic spaces.

above left to right Plates 9 and 10 Dining room in Linley Sambourne House.

The couple's choice of furnishings (although it is likely that Linley, seven years older than his wife and of defined tastes, would have had the deciding influence) was the first indication of the 'artistic' improvements that were to continue throughout their married life. In many ways it was the eclectic combination of very modern and traditional pieces (often purchased second hand from house clearances) that contributed a specific quality to the interior. In this manner a dining suite of almost 'arts and crafts' design and the latest William Morris wallpapers shared space with differently styled marquetry furniture. Similarly, the formal display of photographic prints, which at the time had little precedent, was positioned over wallpaper cut around the picture frames, a conventional Victorian response to the expense of the material (Plate 9).

Significantly for this family history, the Sambourne's collected and displayed a wide variety of objects; bronzes, blue and white Japanese ware, chairs of many styles. Sambourne was to comment later in life, 'What you see is the very best. That has been my principle throughout; not to buy anything but what was really good.'[10] (Plate 10) The interior of the house also bears witness to the needlework skills of Marion. She made curtains, lampshades, sofa covers and embroidered cushions. Two, with her initials, survive in the collection at Brighton Museum (Appendix 28).

Sambourne was, however, not content just to decorate and furnish his home in a highly personal manner; he also commissioned building work, glazing his extensions with painted and stained glass, which provided striking lighting effects, as well as being beautiful objects in themselves. Consistent with his combination of modern and traditional forms, some of the panels depict Sambourne's self adopted coat-of-arms.

Use of the house

By modern standards the proportions of 18 Stafford Terrace might seem generous. However, by the standards of Victorian London's upwardly mobile middle classes it was not considered especially large, particularly when one bears in mind the range of activities – domestic, social and work related that went on there. Unlike many of their contemporaries the Sambournes, though 'comfortable', were not 'well-off' in terms of their income and Linley's chosen career path was never likely to radically alter their circumstances. The family, therefore, set about making the best use of the space they had and there appears to have been no inclination to move at any time during their married life. Indeed, the success of 18 Stafford Terrace as a family home engendered a deep affection for it amongst its occupants, leading in no small measure to its current state of preservation.

Four women servants lived in the house, too – the cook and housemaid in the basement, the nursemaid in the bedroom adjoining the playroom and the parlour maid in the attic. The one other domestic servant, the groom, occupied married quarters rented by the Sambournes above stables in nearby Phillimore Place. It is easy to picture 18 Stafford Terrace as a hive of domestic activity in virtually every room in the house.

Marion built her life around her husband's work and social needs. He was busiest at work towards the latter part of each week and this left him free from Monday to Wednesday to indulge a passion for socialising, sport and dining.

The house as studio

Although it was by no means unusual by the conventions of the time for Linley Sambourne to use the house as a place of work, the extent to which it impinged upon normal daily activity was extraordinary. His extension of the drawing room was not carried out purely for aesthetic purposes. The additional space allowed him to set up an easel and provide storage for the encumbering paraphernalia which supported the production of his weekly cartoon. Sambourne was not sufficiently confidant a draughtsman of the human figure to attempt to draw without a model or some other source image and thus, in 1883, he turned to

Fig. 8 Model posing for Linley
Sambourne, undated.

photography to provide him with a ready supply of source material.
Adoption of photographic techniques enabled him to pose family, friends
and domestic servants into aspects of the proposed drawing.

His wife's diaries record her annoyance, as servants were re-directed
to act as models, often for several hours, wearing various costumes and
draperies, whilst furniture and objects were removed to the garden to act
as props for Sambourne the photographer (Fig. 8). Maud often also posed
for her father. Developing and printing the images even took over the
bathroom and as time progressed, Sambourne's embrace of the medium
came to border on the obsessional. The drawing room cupboards strained
to cope with the storage of catalogued images which by his death
amounted to some 30,000 items.

The house as home

Particularly during the early years of their marriage, the Sambournes were enthusiastic entertainers. During the day Marion received callers from amongst her large group of friends and family, mainly local. Many evenings were given over to dinner parties for up to twelve people. The day-to-day looking after of the children was the responsibility of the nursemaid (Nanny), leaving Marion free to undertake the important task of 'calling'. Marion Sambourne's 'at home' was generally on a Tuesday, when she would receive around four or five visits of two or three people. It remained Marion's central duty to make sure that the household was smoothly run. A good cook was the hardest position to fill and Marion took considerable responsibility upon herself to formulate meals both for family dining and the dinner parties. Formal dinners at Stafford Terrace often took place in burst of activity (no less than five are recorded within a ten-day period in 1880). On these occasions, Marion spent days sourcing menus with cook, instructing the other staff in their duties, as well as worrying about what she would wear.

Life outside 18 Stafford Terrace

The ideal annual round of activities for those who could afford it was a combination of London living with regular breaks in the country. Marion was fortunate to be able to stay, often for several weeks at a time, at the Herapath country home, Westwood Lodge, near Ramsgate. Regular family breaks were taken here throughout the year, along with autumn 'rest-trips' with her parents in Bournemouth. Shooting in Scotland in September was a regular pleasure for Linley Sambourne, one that he took most comfortably alone.

There was little opportunity for the couple to venture abroad. However, in 1890 at the invitation of a friend of Vernon Watney (the brewer), a friend of Linley's, they embarked upon a two-month cruise of the Baltic in Watney's private yacht. Taking in the sights of Copenhagen, Stockholm and St Petersburg, the trip was indeed (aside from a number of excursions to Paris) the holiday of a lifetime.

Shopping for fashion

In order to dress correctly for her busy, annual round of social activities, Marion was obliged to spend much time acquiring her clothes. She patronised top London department stores in central and west London. Nicholson reports that Harvey Nichols in Sloane Street was one of her favourites, but her diary shows that she also visited Marshall & Snelgrove in Oxford Street, Swears and Wells, Dickins & Jones, Whiteleys in

Westbourne Grove, and Shoolbred's in Tottenham Court Road. Barkers and Woollands were only a short walk away in Kensington High Street, and nearby was Harrods, which she deemed in the 1880s to be a 'dirty place though cheap'.[11] Marion was an unsure and fussy shopper and often critical of her purchases. Typical diary entries read: 'Sent back grey dress to Snelgrove, promised to send credit note.' 'Ordered hat which Lin does not like so returned it.' … 'Changed jersey at Marshalls, fits so badly.'[12]

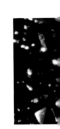

Marion, typically of her rising middle-class status, also ordered her best clothes from local private dressmakers. Their names are not recognised today and most of her garments do not bear a label. However, receipts housed in the Sambourne Family Archive in Kensington Library show that Marion visited Louise Witton of Grosvenor Square for evening dresses, Geo Davis for her Tea Jackets, Judith Rizzo of Bayswater and the Misses Sophia and Kate Weal of the Marylebone Road. Her favoured designer was Madame Bouquet.[13] Marion's diaries also reveal that she visited the fashionable court dressmaker Monteith Young after admiring one of the gowns she had made for her sister. She wrote in her diary in 1897: 'Tabby looking quite lovely in her Young gown'.[14] However, as was often the case with the ever-anxious Marion, when the dress arrived it was a great disappointment. 'Wore new dress, Monteith Young, hate it', she wrote.[15] It was many months before she could bring herself (or was able) to pay the 'monstrous bill'.[16]

Ever conscious of money, Marion faithfully records and comments in her accounts and diaries on the sums paid to her dressmakers, she wrote: 'Went to Madame B's, paid her £38 for making me blue evening dress.' … 'sent cheque £22 Madame B.' … 'To Madame B, asked ridiculous prices, ordered nothing.'[17] This outlay would have been expensive for Marion whose quarterly allowance, as Nicholson clarifies, paid, by her father's estate, was only £25. Maud's sisters, Midge and Tabby, also patronised 'Madame B' and as Nicholson comments it is likely that a sense of pride stopped Marion from admitting that such expensive clothes were beyond her means. She did try employing a seamstress to come to the house for a few days but the results were not up to Marion's nor Madame B's standards. 'Napier here, don't think dress will be a success, shall never fancy myself in anything but Madame's dresses.'[18]

Nicholson has commented that it was Marion, rather than the extravagant Linley, who had to worry about money and sort out financial problems. A list of Marion's assets in 1887 reveals that she received £182.8.10d from allowance, interest and presents, of which £81.1.1.d was spent on dress.[19] The year of Maud's coming-out season, 1893, was a particularly expensive one and so she resorted to using the services of a second-hand-clothes dealer called *Vieux Habits* who discreetly called by the house to buy Marion's old garments, a not unusual (though well hidden practice) amongst middle-class women.

Marion was herself a good dressmaker and serious about her embroidery skills, which she passed on to Maud. Nicholson notes that

Marion sewed a lot by hand but found someone else to do the machining.[20] Marion's early diaries are full of evidence of this, as is the surviving dress collection. 'Worked on pink cotton', she writes; 'Mended dresses and finished home-made black', ... 'Bought Maud's serge and lining for sailor dress 11/-, woollen dress and lining £1.2.9.'[21]

Marion was sufficiently involved in her embroidery work to make the occasional visit to the Royal School of Needlework to buy materials. She kept and made use of even the smallest scraps of fabric and trimmings. One of the boxes of clothing cleared out of Linley Sambourne House was filled with off-cuts (Appendix 29), including five pieces of Morris & Company fabric printed with a foliage pattern, lengths of lace and net, bundles of ribbons and bead and sequined encrusted trimmings, evidence of her frugal creativity.

One of Marion's formal afternoon dresses of about 1885 survives in the collection. Perhaps worn when Marion came out of mourning for her father (who died in 1884), it is an elegant long-sleeved bodice made up in dark green silk-velvet and heavily bustle-backed skirt, made up in a sombre green silk, brocaded with large spots (Plate 11).

Marion's looks faded in the 1880s–90s, most likely due to poor health, as Nicholson has noted. Photographs show her as a thin and

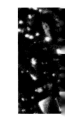

far left Fig. 9 Marion Sambourne, 1910.

left Plate 11 A formal afternoon dress belonging to Marion Sambourne, c.1885.

sickly looking woman with heavy shadows under her eyes. At the turn of the century she put on a little more weight and in her studio portrait of March 1910, when she was fifty nine, she looks a little healthier (Fig. 9). These photographs reveal Marion to be woman no longer at the forefront of fashion, as her clothes are styled closer to fashions of five years earlier.

It would appear, overall, that fashion was more of a chore and an anxiety than a pleasure in Marion's life, certainly in her middle to latter years. Diary entries are frequently marked by disappointment at the garments produced for her, 'Expect black dress to be an utter failure,' … 'Tea gown came, don't like it,' …'New dress arrived, bad' are all her typical responses.[22] Perhaps this was the result of a lack of confidence in her appearance or perhaps displeasure at the expense of clothes, but Marion never sounded excited or even pleased about her new garments or how she felt or looked in them. As Nicholson has commented, only once in her years of diary-keeping do her diaries match the social occasion to the actual dress she wore. She went to a party and wrote 'very jolly dinner, wore red velvet'. A year later she noted down that the red velvet was to be 'done up'. It is another testament to Marion's prudent attitude to spending money on fashion, and also to the particular success of this one red velvet dress, that, ten years later, it was yet again taken to the dressmakers to be remodelled.[23]

Once her daughter Maud (who was always far more confident about her sense of fashion than her mother) reached adulthood, she took on an advisory role. Maud lovingly reassured her mother that she should not worry about clothes as she 'always looks better than anyone else'.[24] In 1913, she wrote to Marion:

My darling, if you want clothes do go and look at the things at Reville & Rossiter. They have their sale and the things are much reduced and quite lovely. I saw some black coats and skirts and dresses but did not dare to get one for you on spec: as I didn't know exactly what you wanted.[25]

This was one of London's top couture houses and there is no evidence that Marion followed up this extravagant suggestion.

Curiously, apart from the mid-1870s silk dresses, few of Marion's best clothes have survived in the Messel Collection, none of Madame Bouquet's grudgingly acquired fine evening gowns, or any garments bearing the label of her other favoured dressmakers. The only couture-level dress of Marion's to survive is the one which she wore to her daughter's wedding in 1898. This is made up in mid-blue silk printed with a fine meandering design in cream and gold and is trimmed with narrow silver braid with blue sequins. This

THE FIRST & SECOND GENERATIONS

ensemble would have represented a considerable outlay by Marion, or Linley, and a willingness to please her daughter. This dress is far more fashionable and less sombre in style than the black, fawn and grey dresses, which she writes about in her diaries and is shown wearing in photographs. This difference appropriately marks the outfit as special occasion piece (Appendix 15).

Two other everyday garments may have been kept because they embodied something quite special to Marion, an occasion on which she was content with her appearance. One is a brown beaver fur jacket with large braided buttons (Appendix 8), which she wore for her studio portrait of 1910, the anticipation of which caused her much consternation. She wrote 'Will look a fine wreck after months of anxiety.' However, it seems she was pleased with the results, writing 'My photos came! Quite nice, wonder if they really are like me.'

In the same group of photographs she wears a black silk bodice with heavy creped strips over the shoulders and inserts of white fabric (Fig. 9). This garment, albeit in an altered form, survives. The white fabric has been replaced by black chiffon, possibly to convert it into a full mourning bodice, to mark the death of Linley Sambourne in 1910 (Appendix 21).

Marion's everyday wear, up till about 1914, survives in quantity – skirts, blouses and bodices for day, evening and mourning, camisoles and nightgowns (Appendix 3–22**).** It would be fair to assume that Marion made some of the simpler garments. Others have been altered and remade and thus have interesting biographies of their own. Marion's clothes speak to us about the domestic life of a middle-class Victorian wife. They survive as testament to both her parsimony and her interest in dressmaking and embroidery, which she passed on with consequence to her daughter Maud and her granddaughter Anne.

The children

Marion's other concern was, of course, her children. Maud and Roy were a fitful presence in the household during their younger years. Nanny took on the majority of what would now be regarded as 'parenting' and primary education under direction from Marion. She would of course spend time with the children but only as other duties permitted and rarely did she take either of the children out alone. Linley Sambourne's involvement with them was even more fleeting. Roy, whose behaviour was becoming increasingly disruptive, was sent away to Albion House Preparatory School in Margate and then to Eton. His father was undoubtedly disappointed that the term 'idle' was most commonly used to describe his son's progress. Roy did win a place at University College, Oxford in 1898, the year his sister married, but left in the summer of 1900 without taking a degree. Put to work in the City his conduct, particularly his (apparently, platonic) relationships with actresses was a pattern which characterised the rest of his life.

Maud was, by contrast, of sweet nature, obedient and respectful. Her parents did not consider a formal education to be necessary for their daughter and so, following the departure of Nanny, Maud was taught by a governess, Miss Gill from February 1889. French lessons were also organised by Marion but none of this was too onerous to prevent the round of 'calling', which would alert suitable families to the emergence of the girl into a young woman.

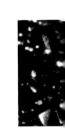

Maud's 'coming out', 1893

Maud was launched on the London 'season' in 1893, aged eighteen. It seems that Maud was quite an attraction. Marion writes in 1894 'To Mrs Thompson's where Oscar Wilde devoted his attention to Maud & was most kind.'[26] However, exceptionally, Maud took time to work at her drawing, at which she was accomplished enough, as Nicholson comments, to have sketches published in *Punch* and the *Pall Mall Magazine*. Maud was paid for her contribution and it is possible that, had her personal and financial circumstances been very different, she could have made a living as an illustrator.

The family was neither rich enough, nor well enough connected socially, to enable Maud to be presented at court as a debutante, though Marion had worked hard to make contacts that would further propel her daughter into society. Maud made an immediate impact upon the eligible bachelors she met at parties and country weekends. She was well aware of her duty. She wrote to her mother of the young men she was meeting, during a weekend at Ayton Castle in 1895, commenting excitedly 'Hardly any of them have less than £7000 a year, so darling, your little own [daughter] may have the chance of fishing out one of them.'[27]

Maud's 'coming out' wardrobe

Her new social life, including country-house visits, required a whole new adult wardrobe. For the first time Maud was taken to an expensive shop to buy an evening dress. The white muslin dress ordered from Woollands for six guineas proved a success when worn five days later at Maud's first London party. Marion wrote in her diary 'April 20th 1893. Lady Reed's dance, 112 Cromwell Road. M looked sweet in her new white muslin, had heaps of partners and seemed much admired.' (Fig. 10)

Significantly, Marion chose to make several of Maud's 'coming-out' dresses herself. Thus, for a socially important visit to the Hampshire home of the Watneys, Maud wore a pink silk dress made by her mother. She wrote home, 'Lady Margaret likes all my little frocks so much.' Maud, already precociously developing her personal style, insisted her mother

Fig. 10 Maud Sambourne, 1895.

send 'a pretty rose pink sash with ribbon to match for my neck and
sleeves … not a meagre ribbon but a nice wide sash – 4 yards.' To
complete this romantic vision in pink, Maud picked a rose for her dress
in her hostess's garden.[28] None of these 'coming out' dresses survives in
the collection.

Maud's engagement

Buscot Park in Oxfordshire, with the Henderson family, was a favourite
weekend destination, but it was an invitation to the Messel country
residence at Nymans in Sussex in 1893, when Maud was eighteen, that
was to re-introduce Maud to her future husband. Despite a number of
other potential suitors, Maud finally did catch her wealthy 'fish'. After a
long courtship, she accepted the ardent and patiently pursued proposal of
Leonard Messel in 1897.

The couple had, in fact, known each other since childhood, through
the family friendships between Ludwig Messel and Linley Sambourne.
This in turn originally derived, as already explained, from the proximity of

Ludwig Messel and Spencer Herapath's offices in the city. It was at a post-Christmas party in the Messel's Westbourne Terrace home in 1889 that Leonard, aged sixteen, first became enamoured of the thirteen-year-old Maud.[29] Nicholson writes that Leonard saw Maud from time to time after 1893, finally proposing to her four years later. At first she refused him but finally accepted. They were married in April 1898, as is detailed in the next chapter. This marriage represented Maud's parents' fondest wishes for a good match for their daughter and confirmation of their own rising status in society. It also proved to be a happy, devoted and fortuitous coupling, which was to last fifty-five years.

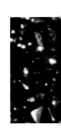

[1] Shirley Nicholson, *Nymans, the Story of a Sussex Garden*, Sutton Publishing in association with the National Trust, 2nd edition, 2002, Chapter 1.

[2] Website of the State Dept of Urban Development Berlin, 25 March 2005.

[3] This survived until the construction of the E-W Berlin no-mans land border after WWII. This in turn was rebuilt in 1994 as the new commercial centre of the Potsdamer Platz. The Wertheim family heirs, now living in New Jersey, USA, filed a successful reparation claim in 2005. Matthew Schofield, 'Jewish heirs to German department-store fortune awarded millions', *Knight Ridde Newspapers*, 5 March 2005.

[4] Shirley Nicholson, *Nymans, the Story of a Sussex Garden*, p. 24.

[5] Ibid., p. 9 .

[6] Ibid., Chapters 2 and 3.

[7] Ibid., p. 44.

[8] Ibid., pp. 6–9.

[9] Shirley Nicholson, *A Victorian Household: the diaries of Marion Sambourne*, Barrie Jenkins, London, 1988.

[10] Proof copy of interview with Linley Sambourne, 1893, Sambourne Family Archive.

[11] Marion Sambourne's Diaries 1881–1914, Sambourne Family Archive, ST/2/1/1 – ST/2/1/35. Quoted in Nicholson, *A Victorian Household*, p. 85.

[12] Ibid., p. 86.

[13] Receipts issued by London dressmakers, 1887–92, 1908–09, Sambourne Family Archive, ST/2/4/5/4.

[14] Marion Sambourne's diary, 8 May 1897, Sambourne Family Archive, ST/2/1/17. Quoted in letter written by Shirley Nicholson to Eleanor Thompson, 23 March 2005.

[15] Ibid., 16 June 1897.

[16] Ibid., 12 November1897.

[17] Nicholson, *A Victorian Household*, pp. 82–85.

[18] Ibid., p. 84.

[19] Marion Sambourne's diary, 1887, Sambourne Family Archive, ST/2/1/7. Quoted in Nicholson, *A Victorian Household*, p. 78.

[20] Nicholson, *A Victorian Household*, p.134 and p. 85.

[21] Ibid., p. 85.

[22] Ibid., p. 84.

[23] Ibid., p. 85.

[24] Letter from Maud Messel to Marion Sambourne, 16 August 1911, Sambourne Family Archive, ST/2/2/1095.

[25] Sambourne Family Archive, ST/2/2/1239.

[26] Marion Sambourne's diary 1894, ST/2/1/14.

[27] Shirley Nicholson, *A Victorian Household*, p. 153.

[28] Ibid., p. 134.

[29] Ibid., pp. 9–10.

CHAPTER THREE

The Third Generation

Biography and buying London fashion: Maud's lifestyle and surviving dress

Eleanor Thompson

The surviving clothes from the third generation of the Messel Collection tell the story of Maud Sambourne's rise into upper-middle/upper-class society, following her marriage to Leonard Messel in 1898. Her etiquette correct wardrobe reflects the range of social activities in which she engaged and reveals her personal aesthetic tastes, which included a love of all that was romantic and picturesque.

The marriage Maud and Leonard Messel

Maud's marriage was sanctified at Saint Mary Abbots Church, Kensington on 21 April, 1898. It was a great social occasion attended by over 200 guests. The *Pall Mall Gazette* reported:

> The wedding naturally excited a considerable amount of interest,
> for Mr and Mrs Linley Sambourne are very popular and number
> amongst their friends some of the most interesting artistic and
> literary celebrities in London, many of whom were present at the
> ceremony and afterwards at the reception held at the Empress
> Rooms, Palace Hotel.[1]

Sir John Tenniel, Bram Stoker and Lady Alma-Tadema were among those invited as well as other famous names from the spheres of the arts,

Detail of dress, c.1905. *See Plate 26*

Plate 12 Maud Messel's wedding dress, 1898.

politics, law and industry. It truly was, as stated in the *Daily News*, a 'Fashionable Marriage'.[2]

For such a momentous occasion Maud's wedding gown (Plate 12), going-away outfits and Marion's mother-of-the-bride ensemble were all designed by court dressmaker Sarah Fullerton Monteith Young, (Appendix 15, 86–88) who had been recommended to Marion by her sister Tabby.[3] The *Pall Mall Gazette* described Maud's wedding outfit thus:

The bride wore a gown of rich white satin Duchesse, made with a short-waisted bodice in the empire style, and arranged most artistically with a collar and sash of fine old mechlin lace; the sash was fastened at the back with an antique turquoise and diamond buckle.[4]

Maud also wore a pretty wreath of wax orange blossoms, a long tulle train and white satin Peter Yapp shoes (Plates 14 & 15). The seven bridesmaids wore 'wonderfully pretty' and 'picturesque' frocks made up in white muslin over white silk with sky blue sashes and large white hats trimmed with ostrich plumes and chiffon.[5]

Maud looked charming and unusual in her high-waisted gown which, in its styling, departed radically from the fashionable pouched bodices of the period. One suspects that Maud chose this romantic style to make herself distinctive. The large antique buckle adorning the back of the gown was a highly fashionable addition (Plate 15). The *Ladies' Realm* in

right Plate 13 Maud Messel's wedding shoes, 1898.

Plate 14 Maud Messel's wedding wreath, 1898.

Plate 15 Buckle on wedding dress, 1898.

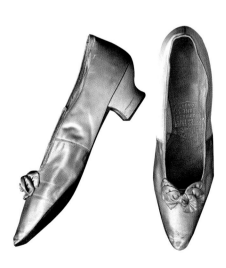

1899 reported the mode for similar antique diamond clasps.[6]

Maud's going-away outfits were of a more conventionally elegant 1898 style, with the addition of some unusual decorative elements. The press reported that:

> The bride's travelling dress was of shot heliotrope voile, daintily arranged with a collar of cream embroidered muslin and *point d'esprit* net, with a pretty little sleeveless coat lined with heliotrope silk and turned back with wide reveres of silk fastened with very quaint pearl buttons. The hat worn with this costume was of heliotrope rustic straw most becomingly trimmed with branches of mauve lilac and draperies of heliotrope chiffon.[7]

As well as this outfit, with its curious opal rosette trimmings, Maud had another going-away costume by Sarah Fullerton Monteith Young, a dress and jacket made up in lightweight pinkish-mauve wool face cloth, trimmed with embroidered floral braid and moleskin. The jacket fastens with two large turquoise scarabs on a gold clasp and chain (Plate 86). The outfit was accessorised with the same straw hat and deep pink stockings (Plate 3).

Married life in London and Sussex, 1898–1915

On return from their six-week honeymoon touring Italy and France, Maud settled into her newly affluent London life. The young couple set up home at 37 Gloucester Terrace, close to Leonard's parents in Westbourne Terrace and in 1900 purchased 'Glovers', a house in the Sussex countryside near Leonard's parents' home at Nymans.

The couple enjoyed a full social life, dividing their time between London and Sussex, with annual trips to Scotland, Ireland and Europe. Leonard was often marooned unwillingly in his office in the city during the week and would write little love letters to Maud in the country, which survive as a touching testament to the private, domestic happiness they shared throughout their married life.

Maud settled quite naturally into her role as wife and a year later as mother to Linley named after her father (Fig. 11). Anne was born in 1902 and named after a grandmother on Leonard's side and Oliver, their younger son, was born in 1904.

Following Oliver's birth, the house at Gloucester Terrace was considered too small, so Leonard bought 104 Lancaster Gate, an ornate, six-storey stucco house overlooking Hyde Park. Here Maud and Leonard had room for their family and numerous servants. Nicholson comments that the move to Lancaster Gate in 1904 set the seal on the young Messel's worldly success. The house was decorated in what she described as 'palatial style',[8] as discussed in Chapter 4.

Charles Castle, Oliver Messel's biographer, comments that Lancaster Gate was to be shared only with friends who enjoyed similar artistic tastes. Anne recollects that 'the people who came to Lancaster Gate were collectors, by and large; museum people.'[9] Among them were Sir Hugh Lane (art dealer and connoisseur), Percy Macquoid (artist), Sir Denison Ross (academic and director of the School of Oriental Studies), Dr W. Archibald Propert, (gallery owner and scholar), Mr and Mrs Gielgud, (Frank Gielgud was senior partner in the Messel family stock-broking firm), and Glyn Philpot, (artist); creative, cultivated, intelligent and wealthy people.

Her husband's wealth enabled Maud to gravitate into upper-class circles and whilst in London she enjoyed a full social life, which included calling upon a specific group of well connected women, such as the Duchess of Marlborough. However, the couple's comparatively modest origins, and Leonard's German-Jewish roots and business activities, may have ensured that they were never fully accepted into the higher echelons of conventional English upper class society, despite Leonard's wealth. Nevertheless, by 1908 Maud had reached a level of society unattainable to her mother, Marion, when she was presented at Court. Writing about the occasion Maud said:

> The Court was lovely … although it was a somewhat lengthy affair … I left the house at 8.30 … some of the servants tried to get side glances at my gown when no one was looking … the queen gave a gracious little bow which I just caught as I made my curtsy to her. I am afraid I did not look at the King.[10]

Maud's presentation dress has not survived, but an undated press clipping reveals it to have been a fashionable white satin gown in the Grecian style, its high waist defined by a girdle of pearls, worn with a small pearl embroidered cloak and a court train of striped silver and satin gauze. An eighteen-foot long train of this description does survive in the collection, which until the discovery of this report was thought to be Maud's wedding train.

Throughout this upward social mobility Maud remained very close to her mother and father and spent much of her time, when in London, with them. Through her parents she and Leonard maintained close links with the artistic and literary circle in which Maud had grown up. Maud's good friend was the children's book writer Gladys Beattie Crozier, wife of Clifford H. Smith, an authority on English antique furniture. Anne remembers that her father 'never spoke about the city … all his conversation was about art'.[11] It is evident that the Messels deliberately patronised young artists, one of whom, Robert Brough painted Maud in 1904 and another, Derwent Wood, sculpted a bust of Leonard in 1905 (Plate 43 & Fig. 24), which will be further discussed in Chapter 4.

Nicholson says that Leonard was by nature private and withdrawn,

Fig. 11 Maud and Linley Messel,
c.1899–1900.

Fig. 12 Maud Messel in morning
room of Balcombe House, c.1905.

more interested in his books, antiquities and the gardens of his country home than in the city or the social scene.[12] Despite a lack of enthusiasm for the stock-broking business, Leonard did very well and in 1902 was awarded a new partnership agreement, which doubled his income. Their increased wealth enabled the young couple to buy a larger Sussex country home. They chose Balcombe House, an early Georgian building set in its own grounds. If Lancaster Gate bore the hand of Leonard, then Balcombe House was very much Maud's creation, the backdrop to her personal sense of taste and style (Fig. 12). In the morning room were: 'High backed William and Mary chairs … rare fire dogs … finely carved bellows hung on ribbons … a set of Neapolitan costume pictures of about 1790 … needlework pictures, silhouettes, embroidered fire screens… .'[13]

It was at Balcombe that Maud and the children spent the majority of the year. Anne, Countess of Rosse's recollection of her upbringing as a young girl there is that it was 'most eccentric … laced with the whims and wisdom of rare parents'.[14] Maud and Leonard engaged the services of a traditional governess who instilled discipline and manners, but the children's true education came from the 'endless stream of specialists and continental teachers who came and went in sequence'.[15] Linley and Oliver were sent to board at Eton, but Oliver, indulged by Maud, suffered bouts of illness, real or imaginary. These kept him at home with his mother and sister. Nicholson comments that all the children were united in their devotion to their mother but Leonard appeared a rather more severe parental figure.[16]

Nymans House

In 1915 Ludwig Messel died, leaving Nymans in his will to his eldest son Leonard. However, the only condition on which Maud would agree to move was that Nymans had to be remodelled, inside and out, to her specifications. Her romantic vision is discussed in the following chapter (Plate 29).

An estate such as Nymans required a large staff, which Daphne Dengate, Maud's secretary companion, says numbered over twenty. Dengate, the daughter of the local vicar, was employed in 1931 and remained in the service of the family until 1994.[17]

Life at Nymans

Once settled in their new home Maud and Leonard assumed the role of the local gentry. Nymans played host to shooting parties and those other rural pursuits traditionally enjoyed by the gentry and aristocracy. The couple were active in the lives of both Handcross and Staplefield, the two villages closest to Nymans. Their status within gentry circles was confirmed in 1936 when Leonard became High Sheriff of Sussex (Fig. 13). Like other benevolent land owners, Maud occupied her time with social calls on her neighbours, being an active member of the Women's Institute, the Mothers' Union, the British Legion and Centre President of The Red Cross. Nymans became a local focus for the war effort in 1914–18 with Red Cross classes held there in First Aid, Home Nursing, Gas Warfare, and Hygiene and Sanitation.

Cultural involvement with the neighbouring Sussex villages offered Maud an opportunity to indulge her creative energies. She organised The Nymans Needlework Guild, the local Shakespearean Society and the May Day festivities on Staplefield Village Green. The first May Day Celebration staged in 1919 must have enlivened village life following the austerity of the First World War. Eric Gill, at the nearby Ditchling Press, designed the programme (Plate 16). Daphne Dengate remembered that:

> [School] children were brought to the common in decorated wagons drawn by horses with bells in frames attached to their collars … A teacher from the Cecil Sharp Society came to teach us Country and Morris Dancing. There was always a procession with characters like …Robin Hood and his Merry Men … The May Queen was crowned after the dancing by the Maypole which was the traditional one with garlands of leaves.[18]

All the costumes were designed by Maud and made by her with assistance from the ladies of the Women's Institute. She insisted that 'the Pageant should be kept with the beginning of the nineteenth century as

Fig. 13 Leonard Messel in uniform of High Sheriff, 1936.

Plate 16 May Day programme designed by Eric Gill, 1922.

Fig. 14 The Tempest at Nymans.

its latest date.'[19] Her vision was that of a romanticised historical past, drawing heavily on a fantasy of the medieval and the 'picturesque'.

Only the Second World War interrupted Maud's staging of Shakespeare's plays, including *A Midsummer Night's Dream* and *Much Ado About Nothing* (Fig. 14). The costumes for these plays were also made at Nymans; surviving family letters indicate that coloured hessian was bought from Barnet & Co, Textile Merchants of Garrick Street, Covent Garden, to make up heavy Elizabethan dresses and tunics. Most of the costumes had to be remade following a fire that devastated Nymans in 1947.

Fancy dress

Fancy dress played a central role in the lives of the Messels. It was a tradition that both Maud and Leonard inherited independently from their parents and which they passed on to their children. Pageants, plays, children's fancy-dress parties, and large fancy-dress balls took place in the Messels' Sussex homes. When in London, the couple attended fancy dress balls, most notably the Chelsea Arts Club Balls, which were organised with involvement from the artists John Singer Sargent and Derwent Wood, friends of both the Messels and the Sambournes. Tom Cross, in *Artists and Bohemians,* has explained that these internationally famous costume balls were hugely popular and lavish events, attended by artists and their guests, celebrities, socialites, leading actors and actresses. Many of the artists made their own costumes and went to elaborate lengths for effect.[20] In 1911 Maud and Leonard attended dressed as Elizabeth Linley (Fig. 20) and Richard Brinsley Sheridan (Fig. 25). Although the costumes they wore have not survived, there are photographs of them wearing them and it is feasible that they may have bought original eighteenth-century costumes for the occasion. This is discussed further in Chapter 4.

Dressing up was undertaken with great spirit and everyone, Leonard included, participated energetically in the activity. Letters from Leonard to Maud in December 1904 excitedly describe the purchases he has made in London for costumes either for a ball or play to be held at Balcombe.[21] Photographs from 1911 reveal Leonard transformed into a mandarin (Fig. 15) and his favourite character, the Whig politician and playwright, Richard Brinsley Sheridan (Fig. 25). These images show a humorous and playful side to a man more often remembered as serious.

Dressing up channelled the family's creative energies. It allowed them to indulge in their personal aesthetic taste for all things 'oriental' and historical, albeit, in a romanticised guise, and it helped to raise their social profile. As Chapter 4 discusses, Maud and Leonard were only remotely connected to Elizabeth Linley and Richard Brinsley Sheridan, but were, nevertheless, able to use this connection to construct a socially useful family heritage and genealogy.

Of the fancy dress costumes worn in the family photographs, just one survives, discussed in Chapter 4 (Plate 41 & Fig. 21).

A number of garments previously thought to be evening wear with unusual decorative elements have been reassessed as unprovenanced fancy dresses (Appendix 65–67). A silver gilt lame and green chiffon dress of about 1908–10 is one such garment. The aesthetic and vaguely medieval style of this gown is of a more dramatic nature than most of Maud's evening dresses and not made to the same high standards. It was probably made by Maud or an unnamed seamstress, possibly for a ball or play.

Fig. 15 Leonard Messel in fancy dress, c.1911.

Maud Messel's wardrobe

The clothing worn by Maud Messel forms the nucleus of the Messel Collection. Almost 200 garments belonging to her were kept after her death. The quantity and variety of clothing acts as material evidence through which we are able to trace her place in society, her style preferences, and the London couture industry from 1890s–1930s.

Almost sixty complete outfits survive, encompassing evening and day wear, and many examples of bodices, skirts, blouses, hats, shoes, bags and other accessories. Most of the garments date from after her marriage in 1898, except for a group of thirty-five items of her baby clothes (Appendix 30). The collection also includes items dating to the mid-1930s. Significantly, nothing survives from Maud's later years. From the 1940s she suffered from severe arthritis and was mainly wheelchair bound, so possibly her clothing in this period acquired a different and sadder significance than the elegant fashion items which have been kept (Appendix 30–159).

Edwardian society was governed by a complex dress code for women. Maud's wardrobe encompasses the array of etiquette correct clothes required in order to be dressed appropriately; morning dresses, mid-morning dresses, house dresses, walking dresses, visiting dresses, afternoon dresses, evening dresses, ball dresses and special outfits for sports and travelling.

The collection abounds in examples of special occasion clothing, predominately wedding and evening dress. This is not surprising, as associated with rites of passage and often involving our greatest capital outlay, it is these items that we cherish. In addition to the many beautiful evening dresses spanning a period of over thirty years (Appendix 57–74), the collection contains Maud's wedding and going-away outfits (Appendix 86–88) and a group of mourning outfits, dating to around 1910–14, most likely related to the death of her father in 1910 or that of her mother in 1914 (Appendix 93–120). These garments reveal Maud to be a highly fashionable and stylish mourner, who followed the convention set by Princess Louise after the death of King Edward VII in 1910, of discarding crape in favour of lighter and more modern fabrics. A group of five tea gowns survive in the collection (Appendix 52–56). These garments would have been worn in the home, privately, both informally and for receptions and receiving guests. Most fashion journals carried regular reports on the latest designs and the correct manner in which to wear them. *The Ladies Realm* stated in 1901 that 'at five o'clock they will don the picturesque teagown and adopt an air of dropping languor which savours of mystery, while striking an Oriental note of passion and colour'.[22] The first of Maud's tea gowns is of pale green silk corduroy lined in brown satin. The second is a voluminous lilac-crêped silk gown trimmed with black velvet, with a cream lace collar, which might have been used for maternity wear (Plate 17). The third, a green

Fig. 16 Maud Messel, far right, c.1905.

glacé silk gown, has a huge cape collar covered with white bobbin lace. Three lozenge-shaped motifs embroidered in metallic threads and glass gemstones are appliquéd onto the back of the garment. A fourth is bright pink silk also with a large white lace collar, and the final and most extreme example is a spectacular gown of layered mauve and green chiffon with a vast train. This is secured to the upper and lower arms only by thin braid bands. This range of styles is testimony to the adaptability of this type of garment and the last exotic and sensual example gives a rare glimpse into the private life of Maud, who would only have been seen wearing this revealing garment by her husband.

Daywear, which is rarely kept, is well represented in this collection through various dresses and suits – classic examples of English excellence in tailoring for women for which London court dressmakers, tailors and designers have been famed since the 1880s. These demonstrate the marked distinction between clothes acceptable for town wear, and those suitable for country activities. In some cases period photographs set the dress into its context. One such example is a walking costume of about 1905 made up in grey wool tweed,[23] trimmed with interesting cut metal buttons (Appendix 39). A photograph of Maud in this costume, accessorised with fur hat and stole, shows her engaged in what looks to be a game of golf (Fig. 16). The roughness and weight of this garment suggest she might well have worn it on her annual visits to Scotland. Interestingly, a walking coat by Samson of about 1907, in what appears to be the same material in the fashionable princess line, also exists in the collection.[24] This suggests that Maud was acutely aware of changing styles and updated even the most functional items in her wardrobe regularly.

Maud's letters and diaries are packed with information about what clothing she wore on particular occasions. A handwritten list of 'things for abroad'[25] in her 1926 diary includes a black and white coat by Reville and a gold coat by Wilson (Plate 18).

Plate 17 Maud Messel's tea gown or maternity dress, c.1902.

Plate 18 Coat by J & F. P. Wilson belonging to Maud Messel, c.1924.

Maud Messel's sources of clothing and the
London fashion world, 1890–1930s

Maud, like all women of her social standing, ordered her best clothes from London court dressmakers, the most fashionable London department stores and from her own private dressmakers.

By the 1890s elite London fashion houses had responded to the social needs of their upper-class clientele by producing tailoring and couture gowns aspiring to those of Paris. Worth, Redfern, Creed and Lucile are international fashion names that live on, but many others have dropped out of the annals of fashion history.[26]

Maud's patronage of these designers began with her trousseau. Her financially advantageous marriage made available to her some of the most eminent court dressmakers and tailors. Sarah Fullerton Monteith Young was clearly her favourite designer, perhaps because this salon seems to have favoured the mildly artistic styles, which Maud preferred. Nine examples of the gowns she made for Maud survive in the collection, all 'best' dresses. As well as the wedding outfits made for Maud and her mother, there is a cream sprigged muslin afternoon dress, with Virago sleeves of 1902–05, the bodice adorned with an antique shoe buckle studded with pink stones (Plate 20). A spectacular evening dress of about 1902–05 in gold tissue covered with sprigged white lace and net has a bodice entirely covered in pendant, quivering fish scale sequins (Appendix 58). There is a dinner gown in the Directoire style made up in cyclamen-pink silk with an embroidered waistband dating to about 1906 (Appendix 58). A cream-coloured satin evening dress of about 1907 decorated with turquoise beading (Appendix 62), a neo-classical style evening dress in green chiffon with a bold Greek key pattern around the hem, is of the same date (Appendix 60). A fashionable purple silk velvet evening gown also of around 1907, has an embroidered centre-front insertion cut from an eighteenth-century man's waistcoat (Plate 21). Lastly, a superbly elegant walking costume of apple-green wool flannel of about 1909–10, is made up in the Directoire style (Appendix 41). The dress is trimmed front and back with jewelled oval buckles and layers of cream net, embroidered with tropical palm trees, boats and cherubs (Plate 19). The matching flared bolero jacket has deep turned back cuffs, revealing a spotted silk lining. All of Sarah Fullerton Monteith Young's creations incorporated interesting decorative features that catered to Maud's preference for subtle aesthetic touches probably designed by client and couturière together, using Maud's antique textiles.

Little is recorded about the exclusive Sarah Fullerton Monteith Young. However, she is known to have traded from premises at 31 Mount Street off Grosvenor Square from 1876–95 and at 65 South Audley Street from 1895–1907 when she appears to have officially retired. Family records reveal that Maud continued to

above, below and left Plate 19 Walking outfit by Sarah Fullerton Monteith Young, c.1909–10.

above and right Plate 20 Afternoon dress by Sarah Fullerton Monteith Young, c.1902–05.

visit Mrs Young for fittings up until 1908, and her apple-green outfit is concurrent with the styles of a year later.

Maud's letters to her mother reveal that she also frequently patronised Mrs Neville. Not much is known about this designer either, who was based in Connaught Street, but it has been suggested (though not proved) that she may have been the sister of Max Beerbohm, Leonard Messel's university friend. Agnes Neville took up dress designing following the failure of her marriage in 1890, and continued until her second marriage to Vesey Knox in 1917.[27] She was known for creating remarkable artistic dresses. Around 1911–13 Maud purchased two dresses from Mrs Neville, both in the slim-line, Directoire style. One is a dinner dress, made up in ivory coloured brocaded silk crepon with a gilt thread waistband with a flower (Appendix 72). The other, an evening dress in white satin is trimmed with gold braiding and thread in an exotic 'oriental' motif (Plate 22). Both dresses are highly fashionable and stylish examples of the Directoire style but not as unusual or aesthetic as those created by Mrs Neville for others.

For over a decade Maud bought clothing from Reville and Rossiter, a more established and conventional salon, formed in 1905 by William Wallace Terry (who took on the professional name of Reville) and Sarah Rossiter, both former employees of Jay's department store. Enthused by a trip there in 1913 she wrote to her mother:

> Beautiful dresses and so fresh. I have bought several things this time. I always go to Miss Mortimer … she is the head woman there, so nice and most obliging. I bought a plum coat and skirt all in silk these reduced from £24 to £14.[28]

Maud purchased day and evening dresses, tailored suits, tea gowns and blouses from Reville and Rossiter between 1910 and 1923.

In about 1902–05 Maud purchased an elegant grey silk outfit with elaborate braiding from Madame Hayward (Plate 24). 'Court dressmaker, ladies tailor, furrier, milliner, corsetiere and ladies outfitter', Madame Hayward enjoyed her

Plate 21 Evening gown by Sarah Fullerton Monteith Young, c.1907.

heyday in London society in the 1910s and 1920s. However, she was a rival to Lucile for the dressing of plays as early as 1898 and was known to be copying Parisian fashions for 'a very few people' in London during the 1900s.[29]

Mascotte of 29 Church Street, Kensington, was the source of a smart and stylish brown velvet and silk chiffon dress of about 1906, with a highly unusual embroidered motif on the centre-front (Plates 37 & 38). Russell and Allen provided an evening dress deemed 'a complete failure'[30] (Appendix 57), Woollands and Wilson were frequented for eye catching cartwheel hats dripping with feathers and bows, Redfern for 'a hat-to-be-rained-on',[31] Liberty for shifts,[32] Samson for a wool tweed jacket (Appendix 46) and Madame Ross for two garments of note – a white satin bodice with a false waistcoat front dating from about 1907 with exotic crewel-work embroidery in a stylised floral pattern (Appendix 76), and a black wool jacket also of 1907, decorated with Russian 'Cossack'-style black braid (Appendix 45). Whilst this jacket seems to be entirely in keeping with the vaguely military-styled walking jackets shown in fashions journals of 1907 such as *The Ladies' Field*, what marks it as something out of the ordinary is the addition of large decorative silver ammonite buttons (Plate 84). London postal directories reveal that Madam [Lizzie] Ross, based at 19 Grafton Street, traded from the early 1900s until 1919 – from that date the company operated as Maison Ross Ltd until it ceased trading in 1941. Like Maud's other favoured designers, the company appears to have produced fashionably styled clothing with unusual and artistic decoration.

Maud's collection includes a beautiful and softly structured tailored

Plate 22 Evening dress by Neville, c.1911–13.

garment bearing the label 'Lucile, 23 Hanover Square'. This aubergine, wool face cloth suit with an asymmetric front and collar and cuffs of brown moleskin dates from 1912–13 (Plate 23). The career of Lucile, the first English couturière with an international reputation, has been well documented. With branches in Paris, New York and Chicago, Lucile designed elegant clothes to meet the social needs of her upper-class society clientele. Lucile was known to christen her creations with dramatic names meant to evoke moods and sentiments. In 1913 she named her long, lean suits like the one in the Messel Collection 'Ishkoodah', 'The Winning Post' and the rather suggestive 'Perhaps'.[33]

It seems that regardless of her frequent visits to France, Maud did not often patronise French couturiers, nor was she impressed with the renowned Parisian style. Despite visiting couture salons during her travels to Nice, Menton and Paris (including that of Jeanne Lanvin), only one garment in the Collection was bought from France, an embroidered white net afternoon dress of 1910 labelled 'Frederique, Rue de La Paix, Paris' (Appendix 34). Letters written to her mother from Paris describe the styles that she observed in a somewhat underwhelmed tone. In 1905 she stated, 'the hats are really caricatures and they are perfectly frightful. The only pretty one I have seen here was on an English woman at the Ritz. All the others look like notes of interrogation and very funny notes.'[34]

In sourcing her clothing, Maud appears to have inherited her mother's discerning attitude towards shopping, Marion's needlework skills and to some extent her frugality. It is possible that some of the simpler and less well-made garments in the Messel Collection were made by Maud or her mother.

Maud Messel's style

The serendipitous survival of so many of Maud's best clothes allows us both to chart the evolution of her style and to set it within the context of contemporary fashion. It is clear that Maud Messel was a highly fashionable woman. She confidently embraced the key stylistic developments during her years of fashionable dressing: 1895–1935, from the S-Bend through to high-waisted Directoire in 1900–1910, from the rising hemlines of the late 1910s, to the straight cut low-waisted 1920s styles and finally to the form-fitting bias cutting of the 1930s. Her awareness of changing fashions was to last her lifetime and was reflected as strongly in her daywear as her evening dresses. Maud's weight and petite frame also remained constant throughout her life and was flattered by her choice of dress.

Maud's clothing of 1895–1905 reflects a strong preference for the

Plate 23 Wool face cloth suit by Lucile, c.1912–13.

Plate 24 Outfit by Madame Hayward
belonging to Maud Messel,
c.1902–05.

palette of mauve, pink, pale purple, pale blue and soft apple green, all fashionable as well as personal favourites. There are a few notable exceptions, one being a strikingly unusual brick-red muslin dress with hand-painted Turkish style decoration outlined in gold styled of about 1905 (Plate 26). By 1910 Maud's colour preferences had shifted in tune with English versions of Paul Poiret's 'Orientalism', to incorporate gold, cyclamen pink, red and rich purple. Maud's fashion choices express an enduring interest in the Far East. Many of her garments incorporate modified oriental symbols, applied as decoration. Stripped from their original context they come to represent a sanitised but exotic and mysterious 'East' which no doubt appealed to Maud's romantic nature and artistic temperament.

The earliest of these garments is an outfit by Madame Hayward of about 1900, a silk crepon, bolero-styled jacket and skirt covered with great swirls of white, mid-blue and dark blue Chinese-style embroidered silk braid (Plate 24). Maud certainly seems to have fallen in love with Paul Poiret's Orientalism, which became his house style by 1908. Her wardrobe contains many delicate, high-waisted, tasselled and brightly coloured chiffon and muslin evening dresses and possibly fancy-dress costumes dating from 1907 14. An evening coat of about 1912 is similar to designs by Poiret. It is made up in back silk lined with mauve silk, with a large shawl collar and cuffs embroidered over what may be a silk *ikat* print and has a bold, gold braid oriental styled circular fastening on the hip (Plate 25).

A group of evening coats dating from the early 1920s fashionably incorporate 'Eastern' stylistic elements. A dramatic evening coat by J. & F. P. Wilson, dating to 1924, of deep red and gilt tissue brocade is figured with large clusters of art deco, oriental-inspired floral motifs (Plate 18). A modish full-length wrap-over coat of dark blue silk is embroidered with an oriental design. This coat by Reville dates from 1923 (Appendix 84). The final example is a loose-fitting coat of fine black silk over a silvery cream-coloured Shantung silk. Its mandarin collar is lined in rabbit fur and the gold ball and loop fasteners are Chinese in style, as are the extremely wide sleeves (Appendix 83). During this period the Chinoiserie style was much in vogue. By 1923 its influence had spread to decorative art, interior and textile design and fashion. It was especially evident in the patterning of fabrics, which were enlivened by embroidered, printed, woven and painted lattice work, dragon and 'exotic' floral motifs which enlivened linear garconne styled garments.

Intriguingly, Maud's collection contains two original Chinese coats dating from the early twentieth century. One in yellow silk brocade and lined in red silk, is embroidered with Chinese figures and large stylised fruit and flowers (Plate 27); the other, in purple silk, is lined in

above left Plate 26 Muslin dress belonging to Maud Messel, c.1905.

above right Plate 27 One of two original Han Chinese jackets belonging to Maud Messel, c.1898–1910.

opposite Plate 25 Evening coat belonging to Maud Messel, c.1912.

monkey fur and embroidered with flowers, foliage and butterflies (Appendix 80). For a lady of Maud's social standing, it would have been inappropriate to wear these Chinese coats in public, since only the most avant-garde or artistic women chose to do so. If worn at all it would only have been in the home or possibly for fancy dress. Most likely, these garments were collectable objects, not fashion items, and their significance will be discussed in the following chapter.

The final example of modified orientalism in Maud's wardrobe is an unlabelled dress and matching kimono-style coat of the early 1930s. The bias cut purple georgette dress has circular a Chinese-style motif woven in gold thread. It is possible that this garment, which also has a waist tie of appliquéd flowers and fruit, was made or adapted for fancy dress (Plate 28).

Whilst Maud's 'exotic' influences are eye-catching, they certainly would not have offended or marked her out as a 'bohemian'. *The Ladies' Field* remarked in 1907 that garments 'Eastern in appearance … introduce the most daring colours with complete success and tasteful results.'[35] Indeed, her adoption of exotic oriental colours and motifs satisfied her wish to keep up to date with the new tones of fashion.

Also woven into Maud Messel's style is a distinct strand of medievalism, in keeping with her general taste, which her daughter Anne has said 'leaned towards the Early and the Medieval'.[36] The most obvious examples of this in her wardrobe are two high-waisted, aesthetic, medieval-style dresses of around 1910 (Appendix 65–66), a completely circular blue velvet cape with pointed collar and beads and jet around shoulders, (Appendix 79) and a cream silk lace dress by Reville, dating to 1923 (Appendix 73), similar to the medieval Italian inspired gowns featured in fashion journals of that year.

Maud Messel's wardrobe in many ways fits the conventional etiquette-correct dress of English upper-class Edwardian women. Maud's clothes display a complete awareness of her place within her specific social group. Appropriately, there are none of the highly formal, lavishly beaded and embroidered court dresses worn by the aristocracy and those who moved in royal circles.

However, it is also evident that Maud used her aesthetic sensibilities and creativity to evolve a personal style that expressed her individuality and fascination with the 'picturesque', within the accepted boundaries of the social world in which she existed. The type of clothing that most effectively describes her style is that of a safely conventional and fashionable dress with artistic touches. *The Ladies' Field* commented on this type of restrained 'artistic gown' in 1907:

> There is generally a time in a woman's life when she absolutely sighs out for a gown which is out of the common – distinguished, artistic. One gets so tired of the ordinary fashion garb, no matter how prettily carried out and the sure knowledge that a hundred, more of less, reproductions of oneself will be present at every crowded gathering, is after a time somewhat depressing.[37]

The garment the journal describes is of a fashionable cut and silhouette with discreet Greek key embroidery, which, like Maud's gowns, is far from the aesthetic and artistic dress worn in the same period by women such as Lady Ottoline Morrell.

A close study of Maud Messel's garments reveals a subtle unconventionality within her taste, manifested in curious buttons, buckles, clasps, touches of oriental style and peasant embroidery. It has become clear that it was Maud who was directly responsible for these additions, applying them herself or instructing her designers to do so. A bill from Sarah Fullerton Monteith Young of 1900 reveals that a fawn morning gown was made up with 'her [Maud's] own embroidered muslin'.[38] It is these highly personal touches, discussed further in Chapter 4, which make her dress more original and individual than other women of her social status, such as Heather Firbank. Through these she developed her simple yet striking picturesque style, which impressed itself deeply upon those who met her: 'I have not told you about the exquisite Maud, the essence of refinement and extravagance. She wears creations that impress one as being childishly simple and unpretentious until one realises how elaborate this sort of simplicity is....'[39]

[1] *The Pall Mall Gazette*, 28 April 1898, Sambourne Family Archive, ST/7/2/25-33.

[2] *Daily News*, 29 April 1898, Sambourne Family Archive, ST/7/2/27.

[3] Marion Sambourne's diary, 1897, Sambourne Family Archive, ST/2/1/17.

[4] *The Pall Mall Gazette*, 28 April 1898.

[5] Ibid.

[6] *The Ladies' Realm*, 1899, p. 770.

[7] *The Pall Mall Gazette*, 28 April 1898.

[8] Letter from Shirley Nicholson to Eleanor Thompson, 30 July 2004.

[9] Anne, Countess of Rosse, 'The Eccentric Upbringing of a Collector's Daughter', unpublished document, early 1980s, Nymans Archive, A/33/2.

[10] Letter to Marion Sambourne from her daughter Maud, 1 March 1908, Sambourne Family Archive, ST2/2/862.

[11] Anne Rosse, 'The Eccentric Upbringing of a Collectors Daughter'.

[12] Shirley Nicholson, *An Edwardian Batchelor: Roy Sambourne 1878–1946,* The Victorian Society, 1999, p. 17.

[13] Charles Castle, *Oliver Messel: A Biography*, Thames & Hudson, London, 1986, p. 18.

[14] Anne Rosse, 'The Eccentric Upbringing of a Collectors Daughter'.

[15] Ibid.

[16] Shirley Nicholson, *A Victorian Household: Based on the Diaries of Marion Sambourne*, Barrie & Jenkins, London, 1988, p. 35.

[17] Daphne Dengate, 'The Memoirs of Daphne Dengate', unpublished document, 2004, Staplefield Village Archive, pp. 13–14.

[18] Ibid., pp. 5–6.

[19] Gladys Beattie Crozier, 'A Village Springtime Pageant' reprinted from *Worlds Work*, March 1927.

[20] Tom Cross, *Artists and Bohemians*, Quiller Press, London, 1992, pp. 59–71.

[21] Letters written at B. Barnet and Co. Textile Merchants, 22 Garrick Street Covent Garden, December 1904, Birr Castle Archive.

[22] *The Ladies Realm*, October 1901, p. 771.

[23] Identified by Bahman Mostaghimi, Head of Woven Textiles, University of Brighton, as a 2 x 2 rough twill tweed probably of Scottish Border manufacture.

[24] Identified by Bahman Mostaghimi, as a 2 x 2 brushed rough twill tweed probably of Scottish Border manufacture.

[25] Maud Messel's notebook, Nymans Archive.

[26] Lou Taylor, 'Mrs Messel's Wardrobe' in Breward, Conekin & Cox (ed.), *The Englishness of English Dress*, Berg, Oxford, 2002, p. 114. Susan North has also made this point in *Style & Splendour: Queen Maud of Norway's Wardrobe*, V&A, London, 2005.

[27] David Cecil, *Max*, Constable, London, 1983, p. 57. Thanks to Caroline Windsor for her research into Mrs Neville.

[28] Sambourne Family Archive, ST/2/2/1239.

[29] C. Shipp, *With A Feather On My Nose,* Appleton Century Crofts Inc, New York, 1949, pp. 79–80. Thanks to Leslie De Bauche and Jenny Lister for their research into Madame Hayward.

[30] Letter from Maud Messel to Marion Sambourne, 28 December 1900, Sambourne Family Archive, ST/2/2/434.

[31] Letter from Maud to Marion, 25 August 1900, Sambourne Family Archive, ST/2/2/413.

[32] Letter from Maud to Marion, February 1898, Sambourne Family Archive, ST/2/2/301.

[33] Lucile design books, V&A archive. Thanks to Amy de la Haye for her research.

[34] Sambourne Family Archive, ST/2/2/654.

[35] *The Ladies' Field*, March 1907.

[36] Anne Rosse, 'The Eccentric Upbringing of a Collector's Daughter'.

[37] *The Ladies' Field,* 1907.

[38] Nymans Archive.

[39] Letter from Leonora Messel, Maud Messel's sister in law to her mother, in January 1904, quoted in Shirley Nicholson, *Nymans, The Story of a Sussex Garden*, p. 34.

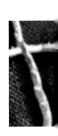

opposite Plate 28
An oriental-influenced dress, early-to-mid-1930s.

CHAPTER FOUR

'Wonderfully picturesque'

Maud Messel's taste for medieval, exotic and romantic fashionable styles, 1898–1960

Lou Taylor

The Messel's architectural and decorative arts interests were firmly in the past. Out of preference Leonard and Maud's choice was for the 'actual' past; an original Charles 1 tester bed or the 'Etruscan vases and a Roman ring' purchased, for example, on honeymoon in Florence in 1898.[1] There are, however, no signs of interest in Art Nouveau, let alone the Modernism of the 1920s and '30s. In this they were typical of many of their class, who, in the late nineteenth and early twentieth century, supported the movement for the revival of English domestic architecture and antiquarian interior decoration.[2] Maud's personal fashion style also drew on the past but only on the terms of the fashions of her day.

Social circles

Maud and Leonard Messel socialised with a mix of wealthy families and with artists and connoisseurs who shared their tastes. Their circles included, for example, the connoisseurs Sir Hugh Lane and Philip Agnew and Percy Macquoid, painter, costume and theatre designer and author of *The History of English Furniture*, first published in 1904.[3] Their wedding gift list includes presents from cartoonists and artists including John Tenniel, Bernard Partridge, Marcus Stone RA and Alfred Parsons,

Detail of man's suit, c.1775–80. *See Plate 45*

landscape painter, watercolourist and garden designer. Walter Crane is also listed, though it is evident that Maud and Leonard did not wholeheartedly embrace the Arts and Crafts movement. Indeed, for Maud at least, it would seem such circles were best avoided. When Maud was twenty one, in 1896, she visited Kelmscott House to have tea with William Morris's daughter May. Maud was shocked by what she saw as the bohemianism of the surroundings. She wrote that the house was 'so artistic, so grubby ... the tea was laid in a barbaric fashion with a loaf on the table and a dirty jam pot that had been broken open through the paper ... Miss Morris [dressed] in such a sloppy way, with no stays.'[4]

Nymans

Leonard inherited Nymans in 1915 following his father's death. The house was not to Maud's taste and so, following her antiquarian fantasies, it was dramatically and expensively rebuilt in the mid 1920s. Its new historical revival design was described by Christopher Hussey in *Country Life* in 1932, as 'an apparently perfect fifteenth century manor house of the kind that one must need go to Somerset or Gloucester to find in its natural habitat.'[5] Following designs by Norman Evill and Sir Walter Tapper, FRIBA, an architect and designer who specialised in ecclesiastical commissions, Hussey reported that during the rebuild 'entire walls with several door heads of a late fifteenth or early sixteenth century were revealed, almost complete to first floor level.'[6] Since neither Maud nor Leonard came from families who had ever owned such property or family heritage, these findings may have afforded them some satisfaction. Hiding behind the historicism, of course, was central heating, a modern kitchen and new bathrooms, one with black and white onyx fittings.[7]

Hussey supportively argued that the new design had been undertaken with 'tact ... scholarship and informed by a sense of the past ... an exquisite example of pastiche – [which] is capable of producing works of art in their own right.' The South Front was styled Tudor, the Great Hall as fourteenth century, and the West Front to early fifteenth century. Hussey was also impressed by 'the quality of the masonry ... [which] repeats the original and is indistinguishable from it.'[8] (Plate 29)

Nicholson confirms that this historical revival building was Maud's own 'romantic vision.'[9] The idea may have grown out of the couple's Italian adventures. In May 1902, antique hunting in Florence and on the advice of Percy Macquoid, Leonard and Maud visited the famous antique dealer, Bardini, in his castle which dated back to 1300. Maud wrote to her mother from the Hotel Grande Bretagne on 2 May: 'This afternoon we drive over to the castle of 'Bardini', a very great dealer ... He is very rich and I fear sells his things at very high prices.' In her next letter to her mother, Marion, she added:

opposite Plate 29 Nymans House.

below Fig. 17 Letter written by Maud Messel, 1902.

Mr. Bardini has not been visible yet, but we have made an appointment to see him tomorrow morning. None of his attendants who show you over know the prices of anything, so they cannot possibly get commissions. I think you and dad would love some of his things, darling. They are quite wonderful – mostly 1300–1400 furniture which looks very out of place with our own very modern things of 1700. There are some chairs we rather hanker after and one of two stools and old chest … The old things look wonderfully beautiful in the old castle.[10]

Maud was clearly very taken both with the romance of the castle and the sight of Bardini's antique furniture *in situ*. She drew a sketch of a chair she particularly admired in her letter (Fig. 17). It is thus not too fanciful to conjecture that visits such as these may have sown the seeds that led eventually to the creation of Nymans as a fully fledged, romantic English 'castle' of Maud's very own. Shirley Nicholson, in addition, suggests that Maud was very drawn by her conviction that her side of the family was connected to Sir Thomas More, King Henry VIII's martyred Lord Chancellor, though this was never proven despite all her searching.[11]

Leonard and Maud Messel as horticulturalists and gardeners

As well as placing their joint energies into the design of their homes, Maud and Leonard both became knowledgeable gardeners and horticultural specialists. Building on his father's work at Nymans, Leonard famously developed the collections of rhododendrons, camellias and magnolias. His daughter, Anne, Lady Rosse, wrote that 'He sponsored expeditions to the East, to American and to Tasmania and Nymans became a … meeting place for all the great gardeners of the day.'[12] (Plate 32) Maud enjoyed arranging flowers and had a serious interest in old English roses, then unfashionable. Nicholson writes that Maud favoured 'soft-petalled, drooping, heavily-scented old roses – whose beauty lasted for a few brief days only – exactly suited [to] her romantic style.'[13]

In 1971, eleven years after Maud's death, her son-in-law, Michael, the 6th Earl of Rosse, remembered fondly that 'Her feeling for plants was essentially sentimental and each favourite had for her its very own personality … she had a magic touch with propagation.'[14] Anne and Michael Rosse propagated plants too and, because Maud adored camellias, in 1970, Nymans produced the *Camellia* 'Maud Messel' in her memory, with its small shapely pink blooms (Plate 30). They also created the *Magnolia* 'Leonard Messel', first named in 1955 just two years after Leonard's death. Nicholson writes that this is one of the most successful ornamental trees introduced since the war, with frost resistant frond-like pale pink and white petals (Plate 31).

Plate 30 'Maud Messel' camellia.

The interiors of the Messel homes

Anne Rosse confirmed that Maud's 'tastes leaned to towards the Early and Medieval and my father's to Continental and Oriental.'[15] Whilst such tastes were not at all unusual for their day, what was exceptional was the Messel's level of connoisseurship, their eagerness to learn from specialists and their assiduous hunting for genuinely antique artifacts. The Messels commissioned the famous interior decorators, Lenygon and Morant to reproduce the interiors from Hampton Court Palace for their Lancaster Gate house, which was hung with 'the finest brocade curtains in the Italian style.'[16] Nymans was less opulent, with its hanging tapestries, beamed medieval hall (albeit built in the 1920s), and polished, worn, wooden furniture strewn with cushions made from antique embroideries.

Collecting

Shirley Nicholson ascertains 'paintings were not [Leonard's] main interest,' apart from a 'Velasquez', which she believes to have been 'of very doubtful attribution'.[17] Hunting for treasures, however, became a

Plate 31 'Leonard Messel' magnolia.

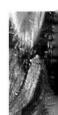

Plate 32 Nymans garden.

joyful lifetime preoccupation for Maud and Leonard. The couple collected everywhere they went. To give just a few examples, in Edinburgh they bought Two luteharps from Mitchell's of Lady Dawson Street, in 1920 for £18.19. In Guildford, W. Williamson sold them English furniture and in Brighton, Stewart Acton of 12, Prince Albert Street, proved a source for furniture, porcelain, glass and pictures. Whilst in the town, they attended the Royal Pavilion Summer Exhibitions. In London they bought various carpets from the 'Anglo-Persian Carpet Company'.[18]

The inventories show that every spring the couple regularly visited Italy (Florence, Perugia, San Remo, Pisa, Naples, Rome and Sicily), as

Fig. 18 Leonard and Maud Messel in Marken, Holland, c.1912.

well as Belgium (Bruges, Brussels), Germany, France (Paris, Vichy, Menton, Nice) and possibly, Lord Rosse remembers, Greece. In the Netherlands, they collected Dutch furniture and were photographed at the harbour at Marken, in about 1912 being pestered by children wearing regional dress (Fig. 18). On all these travels, they bought furniture, textiles, glass, ceramics, musical instruments, jewellery and, of course, fans. Their purchases were packed up and sent after them. Anne wrote 'How well I recollect the arrival of the vans, months later and the childish excitement of my dear parents unpacking them … by the First World War the house [in London] had become a treasure house of the widest possible range of art and beauty.'[19] Typically Maud writes to her mother from Florence on 2 May, 1902. 'We have had such a delightful day … some lovely curiosity shops but the prices are quite beyond us, … Nevertheless we managed to get one or two things. For which Lennie bargained a good deal and came off victorious.'[20]

Leonard as collector

Lady Rosse confirmed that her father's passion for his gardens at Nymans triggered a serious interest in Herbals. His collection became world famous, with some books dating back to the thirteenth century. In the 1980s, Lady Rosse listed her father's other collections – pictures, furniture, silver, rare mounted coconut cups, his world-famous fan collection, oriental ivories, porcelain and early continental glass. A cased Museum Room was created especially for his collections in Lancaster Gate [21]. (Fig. 19) Remembering the fan collection, Lady Rosse wrote:

I can well remember the little Oriental men sent from the famous importer, Franck's of Camomile Street, who came to show him fans … this completely personal attention accounts for the fact that … [the collection] contains no duplicates. Many of the Occidental fans were submitted to him by a connoisseur who was attached to the great Parisian fan making company Duvelleroy with a branch in London.

This collection contained both eighteenth- and nineteenth-century European, Japanese, Chinese, Southern Indian, Indonesian and Korean, folded and screen fans. As Lady Rosse recalled: 'On rare and special occasions we had "fan evenings", reserved for a few intimate friends who were intelligent and cultured enough to appreciate them. My father was prepared to waste no time at all on "philistines" who merely wished to chatter'.[22] Most famously, the collection includes the Dutch or English 'Messel Feather Fan', dating from about 1665, with five standing painted feathers, mounted on repainted, transparent mica panels, 'one of only four presently known in the world' and now rated as a national treasure.[23] (Plate 34)

Fig. 19 Leonard Messel's collection room in Lancaster Gate.

Collecting lace and embroideries

Maud's enthusiasm for collecting and creating embroidery came from her mother and her maternal grandmother, Mary Ann Herapath. Maud developed high levels of expertise on textile history and became an accomplished, serious embroiderer. She searched wherever she travelled for antique textiles – household embroidery, lace, brocade, chintz and brocade curtains, damask napkins and embroidered cushions, even ecclesiastical vestments. She did this from her honeymoon in 1898 for a further fifty years. An inventory of textile purchases from 1902–35 lists the exact sources, types of fabrics and dates of purchase of hundreds of textiles. Dealers' trade cards also survive (Plate 33). At Lenygon, Maud found 'an Indo-Portuguese Quilt' in 1905 and 'Charles 1st needlework valances', in 1924. Street markets were also a favourite haunt. Letters include excited accounts of purchases. Whilst on honeymoon in Venice, Maud writes to her mother on 22 May, 1898:

> We … strolled though some little streets and looked at the shops we went into one, an old curiosity shop where we bought a lovely piece of brocade and a toy for Lennie made in the time of Napoleon and a fan, then walked feeling inches taller for we got the things we wanted with our prices. Then we went to another little shop where I had seen some fascinating little paste buttons. I bought a sweet little collar of old lace and three yards of … old lace.[24]

Maud bought from women dealers in the market place in Florence and visited a local needlework school. She was intrigued here to discover that the thread used was made in Ireland. She carefully wrote down the brand name from a yarn label: 'Linen thread used at needlework school in Florence, Louisa Donalici, via Carlo Bini, 21, Florence / William Barbour and sons / Lisburn Ireland / Best quality.' The 1935 inventory shows that in April 1903, in Naples, for £60 (a major purchase) Maud buys 'two large panels of seventeenth century embroidery and a chasuble in old needlework.' In Rome, in April, 1929, she bought 'embroidered cushions, an embroidered napkin, a sampler and an oval needlepoint sample of seventeenth century embroidery.' In May of 1903 and May of 1905 the Messels were in Paris. Maud buys 'Grecian cushions' and 'six pieces of lace'. Even whilst salmon fishing in Scotland, there was no pause and in Perth, in September 1934, Maud buys a 'piece of Seived work'.

In view of the Messels' love of fancy dress occasions, it is significant that she also buys garments. In February of 1924, Maud purchases an eighteenth century 'chintz dress' from Rosa Dyer in Bath. Records indicate the purchase of four other dresses, not described, at prices between £10 and £1.5.0. On 13 June, 1928, she buys a Georgian silk dress and a pair of slippers from William Mullins, High Street, Salisbury for £22.10.0.

Plate 33 Maud Messel's collection of textile merchant cards.

Plate 34 The Messel Feather Fan. English or
Dutch, c.1665. *Reproduced by permission of the
Syndics of the Fitzwilliam Museum, Cambridge*

Needlework classes

Maud turned her embroidery skills firstly into social occasions and then into a serious educational public commitment. By 1899, just newly married, she set up an embroidery group in her home, with a teacher, writing to her mother 'Half my sewing B today and there were quite a number for Miss Yale and Ethel Clifford came in too and we all enjoyed ourselves.'[25] Maud thereafter ran such classes right through into her old age.

Once established at Balcombe, Sussex, by 1909 she had established formal classes for local girls. Similar philanthropic textile organisations existed right across Europe from the late nineteenth century. Their intent was to provide training and an income for country girls.[26] Daphne Dengate wrote that Maud's class was set up precisely 'for girls who for some reason, like looking after an elderly parent, could not go out to work and it enabled them to earn some pocket money.' At the same time, for example, over in Haslemere, Surrey, craft makers and their supporters were collecting Russian lace and antique Italian textiles, as part of their 'Peasant Arts Collection', for use as design inspiration for their weaving workshop. Maud, similarly, used pieces from her collection as prototypes for her own classes. Daphne Dengate, who became a pupil, recalled the girls 'were taught beautiful drawn thread work from patterns brought back from Italy by Mrs Messel.'[27]

Dengate confirms that Maud's classes started at Balcombe in 1909, with Miss Warren, a teacher who 'was very strict'. Miss Warren, described by Maud as her 'closest companion', had been sent to study at the Royal School of Needlework. Maud enthused to her mother 'The first needlework class went off well and much progress was made and they had tea at 5.'[28] On 18 August, 1910, she noted 'The girls came for their sewing class this afternoon and they are getting on so well. I felt quite proud of them.'[29]

Evidently Maud was involved in selling these products to friends and family, though never through regular commercial outlets, as did other organisations. Work was entered into local competitions. *The Mid Sussex Times*, 21 February, 1911, reported the annual Needlework Show of the Balcombe Association, with ninety-four exhibits, including examples from the Royal College of Needlework. Miss Warren, described as a 'well-known resident of Balcombe', showed her own 'beautiful specimens' of reworked Danish and Jacobean embroidery. The reporter commented: 'We cannot but praise highly the work submitted by Mrs Messel's class', which included 'specimens of Greek and Spanish work'. Maud gave the prizes, and was thanked for 'arranging the class in the parish'.[30]

opposite Plate 36 From top left, table mat and bag made by Nymans Needlework Guild, Casalguidi bag, Chinese bag.

Plate 35 Embroidered bags, linen thread and Nymans Needlework Guild note.

'The Nymans Needlework Guild' and Maud's use of her textile collection

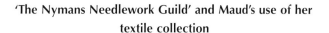

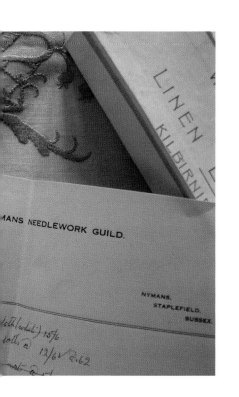

Under the more formal title of 'The Nymans Needlework Guild', classes continued when the family moved house, where the butler served tea to the pupils (Plate 35). Classes of about six women were still being held at Chod's Farm, Handcross, in the 1950s.[31] The retrieval of this lost story of Maud's Sussex needlework workshop, which had survived only in local and family memory, has been another of the unexpected findings within the Nymans archives. Examples of Guild work show its style to mirror Maud's taste, in its simple, elegant character. Three groups of work survive. The first consists of little drawstring bags, inspired by seventeenth-century Jacobean designs. These are small, in ivory silk, with gilt metal drawstrings. One archive example features a peacock design (Plate 36). Maud was photographed in 1911 wearing this with her late eighteenth-century fancy dress and again in 1913 (Fig. 20). Another, decorated with a floral motif, was made by Annie L. Wallace, of Balcombe, for Anne Messel to wear at her wedding in 1925 (see Plate 47). Members of the

Fig. 20 Maud Messel dressed as
Elizabeth Linley, 1911.

Red Rose Guild, a nationwide arts and crafts workshop set up in 1920,
were making more historically accurate reproductions of these bags,
featuring Jacobean meandering rose motifs.[32] The archives also contain a
natural linen bag dating from about 1900, with raised white embroidery,
probably bought by Maud from a cottage industry at Casalguidi, near
Florence.[33] (Plate 36) The second Nymans' style consists of one colour,
silk embroidery on natural linen fabric, in the form of pretty envelope
bags or flat tablemats and runners. Designs are either floral or geometric
and were based on Maud's 'antique' textile samples (see detail in Plate
36). The third type was a range of meticulously made whitework –
reticella, drawn thread and crochet.

Maud, very unusually, placed her own, or her Guild's, decorative
embroidery on to some of her dresses. A patch of 'jewelled appliqué'
work and matching tassels were, for example, applied to her brown
velvet Mascotte dinner dress of about 1906–08 (Plates 37 & 38). This
popular style of embroidery was described in The Ladies' Field, in 1900,
as 'very easy to do, effective and not expensive'.[34] The method involved
layering and cutting away fabrics with infills of sequins and small glass

Plate 37 Evening dress by
Mascotte belonging to
Maud Messel, c.1906–08.

Plate 38 Detail of jewelled appliqué
on Mascotte dress, c.1906–08.

left Fig. 21 Maud Messel in fancy dress, 1913.

below Plate 39 Detail of Maud Messel's muslin day dress, c.1905.

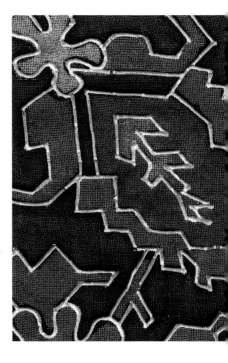

beads. This exactly describes the curious embroidery placed slightly askew on the front of Maud's Mascotte dress. Maud collected antique tassels on her travels, perhaps fascinated by their technical structure. She added brown and gold tassels on the Mascotte dress and hand-stitched green silk ones to her 'Empire' fancy dress of 1913.

Maud occasionally cut up her antique textiles and re-used them directly on her own evening dresses. The most spectacular example is her 'Empire' dress in white satin. Worn for fancy dress in 1913 this has applied gold fringing around the hem and appliqués of embroidered pink carnations and green leaf designs, cut perhaps from a Graeco-Turkish panel, and applied hastily around the hem (some of the tacking stitches are still in place). (Plates 40 & 41, Fig. 21)

Whilst it was common practice in this period to re-use precious old lace on dresses, Maud incorporated both antique buckles and buttons on to her clothes. More mysteriously, and of unknown provenance, is an entirely hand-stitched brick-red muslin day dress with gold braided buttons and colourful, hand-painted, rose and hooked leaf decoration. This is outlined with fine lines painted in gold wax (Plate 39).

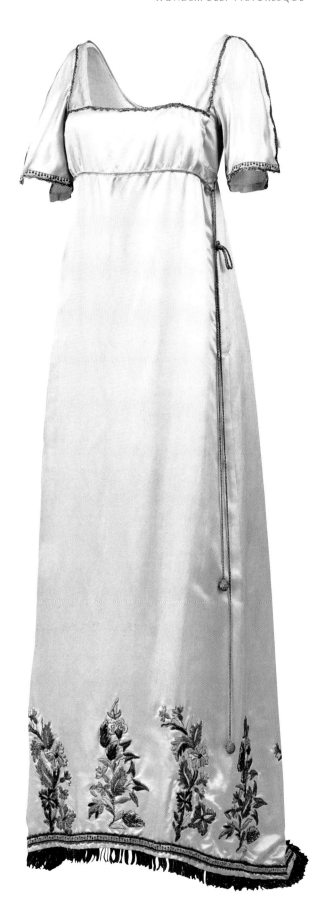

right Plate 40 Fancy dress worn by
Maud Messel, 1913.

above Plate 41 Detail of Graeco-
Turkish appliqué 1913, showing
tacking stitches.

The Elizabeth Linley and Richard Brinsley Sheridan story

This fascination for the antique suffused Maud's romantic fashion choices. Whilst Sir Thomas More may have influenced her architectural preferences, it is clear that the 'Linley Cult' influenced her fashion choices. From Edward Linley Sambourne onwards, the family knew the Linley imagery and in fact sought it out into the late 1940s, even though, as Nicholson confirms, the actual connection to the Linley family is tenuous in the extreme.

The Linley cult built up around the true story of the elopement of Elizabeth Linley and Richard Brinsley Sheridan in 1772. Elizabeth, from an extraordinarily musical Bath family, was a highly talented classical singer by the age of sixteen. Lewis Gibbs writes that she was invited to sing 'at the Queen's Concert at Buckingham House' in 1773. Sheridan, who was born in Dublin, became a famous Whig politician, MP for Stafford from 1780 and is described by Lewis Gibbs as a witty and charming 'social companion' to the aristocracy, including the Prince of Wales. He was, of course also an extremely successful dramatist and manager of the Drury Lane Theatre. His plays, including *The Rivals* (1775), and the *School for Scandal* (1777), have remained constants in the literary firmament and in theatre repertoires ever since.

Sheridan first met Elizabeth when she was sixteen and he, twenty one.

Fig. 22 John Russell, Richard Brinsley Sheridan, 1778.
National Portrait Gallery, London

Plate 42 Thomas Gainsborough, Mrs. Richard Brinsley Sheridan 1785–87.
Andrew W. Mellon Collection
Image © 2005 Board of Trustees
National Gallery of Art, Washington D.C.

She was already by then as celebrated for her extraordinary beauty as for her singing. In 1772, in order to avoid a scandal caused by an unwise relationship with a Major Mathews, (who unknown at first to Linley, was married,) she eloped to France with Richard Brinsley Sheridan as her protector. They married secretly, and on returning to England, Sheridan fought two duels with Mathews. Eventually Elizabeth and Sheridan married, and although Sheridan had no income, they lived as celebrities, extravagantly, in the fashionable world.[35] Elizabeth was painted many times, often by Gainsborough, including his portraits of 1773 and 1785. The second, highly romantic painting, shows her seated, hatless, beneath a tree, wearing a fashionable chemise *à la reine* (Plate 42). In 1788 John Russell produced a sensitive pastel drawing of Sheridan (Fig. 22) and a year later Sir Joshua Reynolds painted Sheridan's portrait.

The Linley cult

In 1988, Giles Waterfield, Director of the Dulwich Picture Gallery, curated a fascinating exhibition which explored the lives and lasting legacy of the Linley family, 'A Nest of Nightingales, Thomas Gainsborough and the Linley sisters.' He writes that a Linley cult developed through the impact their story had on the imagination of artists and the public from the mid-nineteenth century onwards. Waterfield linked this vogue to the Victorian/Edwardian revival of interest in late eighteenth-century English portraiture.[36] Thus Gainsborough's *Miss Linley*

Fig. 23 Jeremiah Barrett Sheridan, Assisting Miss Linley In Her Flight From Bath, 1860.
Brighton Museum and Art Gallery

of 1773 was bought by Philadelphia Museum of Art in 1903. There was, too, a popular vogue for historical genre painting over the 1850–1910 period. Jerry Barrett, for example, painted a romanticised vision of *Sheridan Assisting Miss Linley on her Flight from Bath,* exhibited at the Royal Academy in 1860 (Fig. 23) and now in the Brighton Museum collection. The Messel's friend, Marcus Stone, was just such a genre painter, as was Talbot Hughes, whose antique dress collection was donated to the Victoria and Albert Museum in 1913.[37]

The Messels and the Linley cult

The Sambournes and Messels were, rightly or wrongly, able to pull out an ancestral connection to Elizabeth Linley. In 1911, the same year that Maud and Leonard attended the Chelsea Arts ball dressed as Linley and Sheridan, Clementina Black, suffragist, and fighter for the rights of needlewomen, published her study 'The Linleys of Bath'. Waterfield quotes her conclusion. 'The charm that belonged to so many of them has not wholly died with them; it seizes those persons through whose hands their letters pass … or those who look upon their portraits.' [38] These words could exactly describe Maud's reaction to the life of the talented, beautiful Elizabeth Linley. They also aptly describe Maud's own charming, fancy-dress interpretations of Linley.

Maud's interest in Elizabeth Linley was active, personal but also fashionable. The family kept a cutting from *The Sphere* of 1903, noting the death of the artist Margaret Isabel Dicksee (daughter of the painter of Thomas Francis Dicksee), illustrated with a print of her painting 'The Linley sisters sing, their brother plays the piano and Sheridan watches.' The whereabouts of this painting is not at present known.

1904–05 was a key period in terms of Maud and Leonard's fascination for this story. At this time they moved to Lancaster Gate and commissioned Linley-Sheridan related portraits from two young, talented and rising artists, a portrait of Maud by the Scottish painter, Robert Brough in 1904 (Fig. 24), and a small bronze bust of Leonard, from the sculptor Francis Derwent Wood in 1905 (Plate 43).

We know from surviving photographs that the portrait hung in a place of honour in the drawing room of the London house, before its later removal to Nymans, where it was destroyed in the house fire of 1947. Brough was a friend and admirer of the artist John Singer Sargent and shared his Chelsea studio. Soon after Brough had completed Maud's portrait, he was severely injured in a railway accident near Sheffield on 21 January, 1905. He died a few days later, at the age of only thirty three. The whole family was deeply shocked at the news. Maud wrote to her mother from Balcombe House, where the portrait may have been painted: 'everything here so recalls him – and we both feel it terribly. His life was so full of promise and he was such a delightful companion and friend

Plate 43 Derwent Wood bust of
Leonard Messel, 1905.

that it will be a loss to all those who knew him.'[39] Sargent and Sir Charles Holroyd, Director of the National Gallery, organised a memorial exhibition at Burlington Fine Arts Club in 1907. Maud's portrait was borrowed. The catalogue entry provides a detailed description:

> Portrait of Mrs L.C.R. Messel, property of L.C.R. Messel, Esq. Lancaster Gate, London. W. Life-size, half length, standing, almost full face, the head slightly tilted to *r*. She wears a white dress, cut low, pale blue sash, and a large grey hat tied under the chin with broad brown ribbons which she holds in the cleft of her left fingers and lets fall in front of the figure. Dark blue background. Unsigned. Painted 1904. Canvas. Oil. 39in. by 30in.[40]

The styling of this portrait exactly reflects Maud's appropriation of Elizabeth Linley's style, in its colours and romantic fusion of 1780s and 1900 fashions. Maud's waved hair is fashionable to 1904 but her sashed dress resembles the *chemise a la reine* in the Linley portrait of 1785, and her wide brimmed hat is found in many portraits of English women dating from the 1780–85 period.

In 1905 Leonard also commissioned a bronze bust of himself, from Francis Derwent Wood, a friend of Linley Sambourne.[41] In this small, elegant sculpture, Leonard is shown, too, wearing 1780s clothes, including a wig, cravat and jacket, similar to the Reynolds and Russell portraits of Sheridan of 1788–89. The sculpture survives in the family collection.

Fig. 24 Robert Brough portrait of
Maud Messel, 1904.

Late eighteenth-century influences on women's fashions: 1900–1910

Oliver Messel remembered that 'My darling mother, always [had] the eye for the picturesque.'[42] What is evident here is that by the time of Maud's wedding in 1898, her 'picturesqueness' was also fashionable, certainly in London where styles may have differed somewhat from high couture styles in Paris. By then these were heavily enmeshed in Art Nouveau decoration. *The Lady's Realm* of 1899 commented, 'We remain faithful to the Louis XVth design.' Maud slipped close to the edge of eccentricity in support of this fashion when she inserted a triangle of embroidered silk cut from a man's late eighteenth century waistcoat into the centre front of an otherwise conventional, Fullerton Monteith Young purple velvet, dinner dress of 1906–08.[43] (see Plate 21) Maud's pink going-away hat, with its dove's wings and lilac fronds, trod a more conventional path between the contemporary and the historic (see Plate 3). *La Mode Illustrée* of May 1901 featured a similar 'Directoire' hat, by Mme Boitté, 3, Rue D'Alge, Paris, in black straw with the same pink lilac flowers. *The Lady's Realm* of 1899 described fashionable hats in words which directly mirror Maud's 'look' in the Brough portrait:

> The most beautiful hat ever created is undoubtedly the 'Gainsborough' or Sir Joshua Reynolds, style of headgear ... This class of hat with its lovely curves and lines, ... can never fail to be ... picturesque ... Poised at the exact angle, on soft waving tresses, carelessly but most artistically arranged, and accompanied by a girlish or dignified beauty, the effect is perfect. [44]

Fancy dress

Maud and Leonard fully indulged their appropriation of the Linley/Sheridan style on fancy dress occasions, as photographs of 1911 reveal. One shows Leonard complete with three-cornered hat and another in a wig and a different deep-cuffed coat (Fig. 25). Writing on the back of the photograph confirms that they were indeed dressed as Elizabeth and Sheridan for the Third Arts Club Ball at the Albert Hall in that year. Their Linley interest continued unabated after the Great War. The 'Georgian' dress Maud bought in 1928 in Salisbury survives still. In excellent condition, this is a cream-coloured, Spitalfields silk, dress of about 1780, brocaded with rosebud motifs (Plate 44).

Orientalism

A second, strong decorative arts influence runs through the Messel's life – orientalism. As we have seen, Maud's wardrobe reflected this fashionable

Fig. 25 Leonard Messel dressed as Richard Brinsley Sheridan, 1911.

vogue from about 1912 into the late 1920s. After her marriage to
Leonard, a connnoisseur's orientalism had, anyway, been part of her life,
through her husband's collections of Asian trees, Chinese ceramics,
Japanese *netsuke* and his Oriental fans. Maud collected large
embroidered Chinese, drawstring bags (Plate 36). The couple were close
friends with Dr W. Archibald Propert, supporter of Diaghilev and the
Ballets Russes, whose book *The Russian Ballet in Western Europe,
1909–1920* came out in 1921.[45] It is of little surprise to find that they held
their own Arabian Nights Ball at New Year in 1912 in Balcombe House.
Kathleen Owens, their gamekeeper's daughter recalled sneaking a view
through an open door. 'I can still remember a ball with an Eastern themes
and the beautiful jewel colours of the dresses.'[46]

It seems unlikely that Maud, on such an occasion, would have
departed too far from her personal style and no evidence survives to
suggest she wore Chinese dress. However, Leonard certainly did, as is
seen in a photograph of him in Chinese robes, with beads, hat and false
glasses and moustache. On the back Maud has written 'Lennie in
Mandarin costume' (see Fig. 15). The family owned two Han Chinese
women's jackets (Plate 27) dating from the 1890–1915 period, brought
back from China by Maud's uncle, Edgar Herapath,[47] who travelled there
in 1904, and 1913–14[48] but there is no evidence that Maud ever wore
these (Appendix 81–82).

Plate 44 Detail of Maud Messel's
Spitalfields silk dress, 1780.

Fire at Nymans, 1947

Maud and Leonard's lives in London and Sussex kept the same pattern through the interwar period but all this was shattered by an uncontrollable fire at Nymans on a cold winter night of 1947. Water froze in the firemen's hosepipes and nothing could be done to stop the blaze (Fig. 26). Maud's portrait by Brough, the children's by Glyn Philpot and the 'Velasquez' were burnt. So too were all Leonard's precious Herbal books and all his research notes. Over 100 items of furniture, tapestries and ceramics were saved, however, and Leonard asked that a picture of his mother Annie be bought out as the fire raged.[49]

Fig. 26 After the fire at Nymans, 1947.

Fig. 27 Samuel Cotes miniature of
Elizabeth Linley, 1778
*Private Collection, Photograph:
Photographic Survey,Courtauld
Institute of Art.*

Plate 45 Detail of Leonard Messel's
century suit, c.1775–80.

Replacement goods were bought in the late 1940s, including pieces
from London jewellers for Maud. The loss even triggered a final bout of
Linley\Sheridan collecting. Lord Rosse suggests this was to regain their
spirits after the shock of the fire. After the event, Leonard bought a
precious c.1778 miniature of Elizabeth Linley by Samuel Cotes, one of
England's foremost miniaturists, a gentle watercolour on ivory,[50] (Fig. 27)
and a man's suit, dating from about 1775–80. The label attached reads:
'This suit was formerly the property of Lord Carnarvon, Highclere Castle.'
It may be French and is made in brown silk. The jacket is embroidered
with floral sprays in green, white and pink, and has matching velvet knee
breeches. The waistcoat is in white satin, embroidered in coiled, silver
metallic thread in a scrolled pattern with large paste glass buttons
mounted in silver (Plate 45).

This was purchased from Charles Angell, 'Antiques – Works of Art,'
34, Milsom Street, Bath, on 10 May, 1948, after an auction at Highclere
Castle, Newbury, the family home of the Carnarvon family, on 19 March,
1947.[51] [52] It is possible that this suit was worn by Henry Herbert, 1st Earl
of Carnarvon (1741–1811). It was his descendant, the 5th Earl,
(1866–1923) who discovered the tomb of Tutankhamen in the 1920s. In
1947, the 6th Earl was married to Tilly Losch, the ballet dancer and
actress, ex-wife of Edward James. Some of her 1929 theatre costumes had
been designed by Oliver and made by Anne Messel.[53]

This purchase could also be connected to Oliver Messel's work. By then he was internationally famous for his fantastical recreations of the Sheridan/Linley period of the eighteenth century. Two years before the fire, Oliver had completed sets and costumes for Sheridan's *The Rivals*, starring Edith Evans and Anthony Quayle, at the Criterion Theatre, London. At the time of the purchase of this suit, Oliver was working on Mozart's *The Magic Flute* for Covent Garden. He repeated his triumph again at Glyndebourne for the *Marriage of Figaro* in 1955 and again in later productions. There is no doubt that the whole family would have been entranced by the splendour, history and quality of this suit.

However, despite the best efforts of everyone, the consequences of the fire took a heavy toll on Leonard and Maud. Maud was seventy two and Leonard seventy five. Anne remembered her husband taking Leonard over to Nymans, 'to see the new plantings – but never going near the house.'[54] The couple moved to Holmstead Manor nearby and never lived in Nymans again. Leonard died in 1953 and Maud in 1960.

[1] Letter from Maud Messel to Edward Linley Sambourne, 1898, Sambourne Family Archives, ST/1/2/1223.

[2] This movement is typified in Ernest Willmott's study *English House Design – a review*, Batsford, London, 1911.

[3] His widow bequeathed part of his collection of art, furniture, silver, pictures and porcelain to Preston Manor, Brighton.

[4] Shirley Nicholson, *A Victorian Household*, Sutton Publishing, Stroud, 1998, p. 154.

[5] Christopher Hussey, 'Nymans, Sussex, The Residence of Lieutenant Colonel Messel', *Country Life*, 10 September 1932, p. 297.

[6] Ibid., p. 294.

[7] With thanks to Rebecca Graham, House Manager, Nymans House, National Trust.

[8] Christopher Hussey, p. 294.

[9] Shirley Nicholson, *Nymans, the Story of a Sussex Garden*, Sutton Publishing and the National Trust, Gloustershire, 2001 p. 69.

[10] Sambourne Family Archives ST/2/2/527.

[11] Letter to Eleanor Thompson, 30 July 2004.

[12] Anne, Countess of Rosse, 'The Eccentric Upbringing of a Collector's Daughter', unpublished document, early 1980s, Nymans Archive, A/33/2.

[13] Shirley Nicholson, *Nymans*, p. 67.

[14] Shirley Nicholson. *Nymans*, p. 93, quoting a text from a Royal Horticultural Society lecture, given by Michael, Lord Rosse at Nymans in 1972.

[15] Anne Rosse, 'The Eccentric Upbringing of a Collector's Daughter'.

[16] Ibid.

[17] Letter to Eleanor Thompson. 30 July 2004.

[18] Inventory of about 1935, Box 53, Nymans Archives.

[19] Anne Rosse, 'Leonard Messel, The Collector and the Man 1872–1953', article for the Fan Circle. Undated, probably mid-1980s, Birr Archives.

[20] Sambourne Family Archive, ST/2/2/527.

[21] Anne Rosse, 'My Father the Collector.'

[22] Ibid.

[23] Fitzwilliam Museum, *Fans from The Fitzwilliam – a selection of the Messel-Rosse collection*, The Fitzwilliam Museum, Cambridge, 1985. p. 12.

[24] Sambourne Family Archives, ST/2/2/313.

[25] Sambourne Family Archives, ST/2/2/398.

[26] See Wendy Salmond, *Arts and Crafts in Late Imperial Russia*, Cambridge University Press, Cambridge, 1996 and Tanya Harrod, 'For Love and Not Money, Reviving Peasant Art in Britain, 1880–1930', in David Crowley and Lou Taylor, *The Lost Arts of Europe – The Haslemere Museum Collection,* Haslemere Educational Museum, 2000.

[27] 'The Memoirs of Daphne Dengate', unprovenanced typed script, c.2004. Village Archives, Staplefield, p. 6.

[28] Sambourne Family Archives, ST/2/2/965.

[29] Sambourne Family Archives, ST/2/2/1034.

[30] Ibid.

[31] Interview by the author with Miss Rowe, Handcross, 2004.

[32] See embroidered bag, made by Kathleen Clarke, Wimslow, for the *Red Rose Guild of Art Workers, The Studio Year Book of Decorative Art*, London, 1925, p. 120.

[33] With thanks to Lynn Szygenda of the Embroiderers' Guild for this identification.

[34] *The Ladies' World*, 1900, vol. 2, pp. 929–30.

[35] Lewis Gibbs, *Sheridan*, Dent, London, pp. 4, 6, 31.

[36] Giles Waterfield, *A Nest of Nightingales, Thomas Gainsborough and the Linley Sisters*, Dulwich Picture Gallery, 1988, pp. 35–38, 37.

[37] Lou Taylor, *Establishing Dress History*, Manchester University Press, Manchester, 2004, Ch. 4.

[38] Waterfield, *A Nest of Nightingales,* p. 38, quoting Clementina Black, *The Linleys of Bath*, 1911, pp. 291–92.

[39] Letter from Maud Messel to Marion Sambourne, 22 Jan 1905, Sambourne Family Archive, ST/2/2/648.

[40] Catalogue of the exhibition of works by Robert Brough, Burlington Fine Arts Club, London, 1907, p. 12.

[41] Letter from Linley Sambourne to Derwent Wood on Woods election to the Royal Academy, 17 January 1910, Sambourne Family Archive, ST/1/4/1072.

[42] Giles Waterfield, p. 20.

[43] Eighteenth-century waistcoats were included in the last Nymans sale by Sotheby's in 1994.

[44] *The Lady's Realm* , 1899, Vol. 1, p. 430

[45] W.A. Propert, *The Russian Ballet in Western Europe, 1909–1920,* John Lane, London 1921.

[46] Kathleen Owens, as told to Joy Madwick, *The Tale of the Gamekeeper's Daughter*, 2002, Nymans Archives, 77/9(i).

[47] Sambourne Family Archives, ST/2/2/1631;ST/2/2/1741; ST/2/2/1628, with thanks to Eleanor Thompson.

[48] With thanks to Verity Wilson for kindly identifying these.

[49] With thanks to Rebecca Graham, House Manager, Nymans Archives

[50] The V&A has a miniature by Samuel Cotes, 1734–81, *Portrait of an Unknown Man,* dated 1757 (Museum no. P.8-1929).

[51] This sale was conducted by Drewett, Watson and Barton. With thanks to Mrs J. Thorp, Archivist, Highclere Castle and Eleanor Thompson.

[52] Thanks to Eleanor Thompson for this research.

[53] Castle Charles, *Oliver Messel, A Biography*, Thames and Hudson, London, 1986, p. 46.

[54] *Woman's Weekly*, 7 September 1985, p. 53.

CHAPTER FIVE

The Fourth Generation

History and Narrative: Anne Messel's style and evolving dress collection

Amy de la Haye

Mrs Armstrong-Jones can wear a beret and, with her flying capes and her debonair manner, your immediate impression is not so much of any particular fashion … as of the cavalier spirit in every age: although all her clothes taken by detail are in the latest possible mode. (*Evening News*, 1931)[1]

As a young woman, Anne Messel developed a distinctive personal style which, like that of her mother, Maud, was inspired by a passion for romanticism, history and flowers. These influences are not only evident in her meticulous selection of fashionable clothing and accessories and the designers who created them, but also in her carefully studied choice of fancy-dress persona and representation within portraiture. Like Maud, Anne also made and individualised her own clothes, creating a unique personal expression.

The fashionable dresses that Anne selected, made, embellished, wore and subsequently preserved are laced with biographical references, many of which have roots in her childhood and echo her parents own preoccupations. Anne's surviving clothes from this period tell stories which make explicit her passion for romanticism, history and flowers.

Detail of 'Ribbon dress' by Charles James, 1939. *See Plate 53*

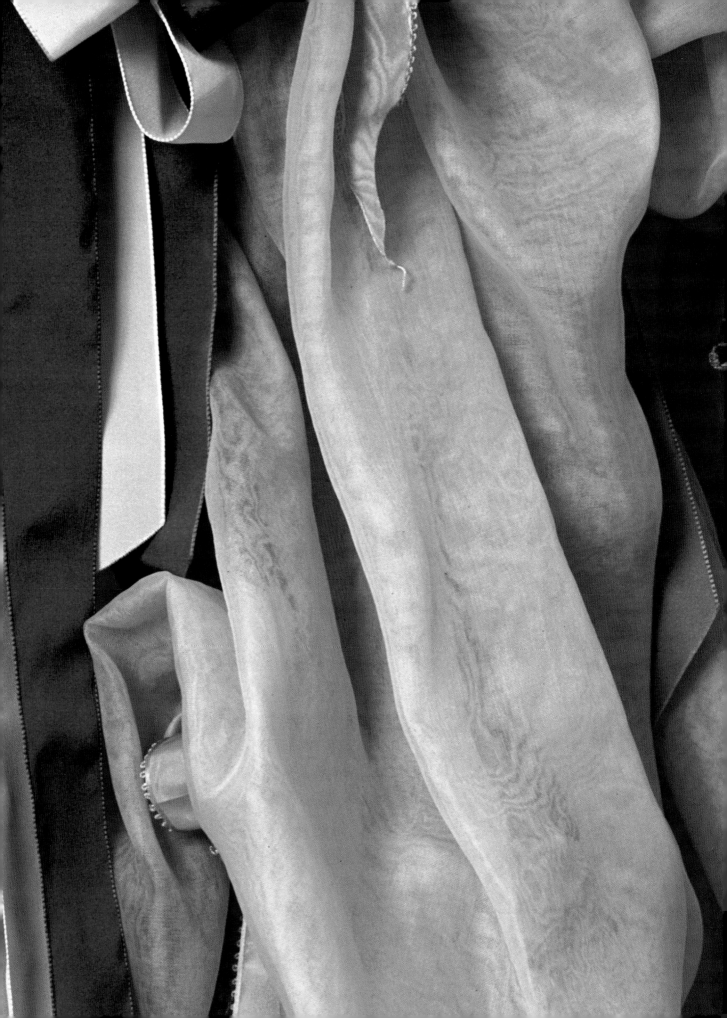

Enchanted childhood

An understanding of Anne's upbringing sheds light upon the distinctive style she developed and for which she was to receive widespread admiration. As described in previous chapters, Anne and her brothers Oliver and Linley grew up in a household where creativity, imagination and beauty were highly prized. Anne wrote to Charles Castle:

> The people who came to [our houses at] Balcombe and Lancaster Gate were collectors, by and large; museum people. And therefore museums came into our lives very early on. Oliver and I started being taken to the V&A as small children – which was my only real schooling.[2]

Fig. 28 Anne and Oliver Messel in fancy dress, c.1910.

Like Maud, Anne was educated at home whilst the boys were sent to Eton. However, prior to this the trio were together taught a variety of creative skills at home. In a talk Anne gave to the Fan Circle entitled 'The Unconventional Upbringing of a Collector's Daughter', she recalled being taught the art of early weaving:

> Our teacher was an eccentric old woman dressed as a shepherd, smock and leggings and all, and speaking as a man in brogue … How vividly these escapades linger in my mind: the collecting of dirty sheep's wool from the hedges, the washing, the carding, the spinning and finally the weaving … Every form of needlework was a joy, from lace-making taught by a nun to Umbrian needlepoint from a charming Italian. And woven through it all was the whirl of languages, music, paintings and singing. But where did Geometry, Algebra and Higher Mathematics come in? Nowhere, alas! So there would be no chance of O or A levels.[3]

Throughout their lives Anne and Oliver had shared interests and were very close. Anne told Castle:

> There were months when we were in bed. We both had a bit of tuberculosis. At least we thought we had. And that was really when we made so much with our hands. We'd sit up in bed making things: little maquettes, perhaps a chapel. Little candlesticks, altars and satiny bishops, all dressed up, because we both loved sewing.[4]

Two mornings each week the children were taught gardening skills at Nymans, and Anne discovered a pastime for which she developed a lifelong passion and in which she was, like her father, to become highly accomplished. As her surviving garments reveal, her love of plants and colourful flowers was closely reflected in her choice of floral dress fabrics, whether printed, woven or embroidered, and her love of corsage (floral decoration – real or artificial – applied to a garment).

The Messel children also spent extended periods without any form of schooling, at which time they amused themselves with games and activities in which their vivid imaginations and love of fantasy could take a free reign. Dressing-up was a favourite pastime: Oliver's earliest childhood memory went back to when he was about four years old and dressed as a French soldier.[5] Archival photographs capture him dressed as Cupid with crêpe wings, or as a harlequin, and Anne in ethereal muslin frocks with either flowers in her hair dressed as a May Queen (Fig. 28), or with her own wings.

As adults, Anne and Oliver would retain their childhood delight in fantasy and fancy dress. Following their mother's example, Anne became an accomplished embroiderer, and created domestic pieces as well as making and embellishing her own, and later her daughter Susan's, clothing. Oliver became internationally acclaimed for his set and costume designs for theatre, opera and film. Linley studied at Cambridge before becoming a stockbroker in the family firm. By the mid-1920s Oliver, and later the Anglo-American couturier Charles James, drew on Anne's skills to realise their professional dress designs.

Fig. 29 Anne Messel's presentation photo, 1922.

Anne and Oliver enter London society

Anne and Oliver's introduction into fashionable society in the early 1920s coincided with a gradual change in the fabric of elite social life and a re-structuring of London's fashion industry. Anne came out as a debutante in 1920, when she was eighteen years old, but was not formally presented at court until June 1922 (court presentations had been suspended for the war and early post-war years) (Fig. 29). The function of the season had changed little from Maud's day, although there was greater informality. During that and subsequent summer seasons Anne lived at Lancaster Gate and attended the round of parties, dances and events that constituted the British social season, retreating to Nymans to enjoy country life. Nicholson writes: 'Small and lively, enchantingly pretty and indulged by doting parents with everything that money could buy, she was soon surrounded by a host of admirers.'[6]

One of the evening dresses Anne wore at this time is made from gold tissue mounted on dark red silk with a bodice of flesh-toned muslin. The skirt is overlaid with gilt lace, reinforced with brown lace and studded with small diamante (Plate 46). Dating from about 1924, it is not attributed to a particular designer. There is plenty of photographic evidence that shows Anne wearing *sportive garçonne* styles during the daytime (Fig. 30), but none of this survives. Although this style did not emphasise the tiny waist of which Anne was so proud, her choice of materiality was rich and ornate, the overall impact overtly feminine. This dress is the earliest item of her own clothing that Anne preserved, and it formed the basis of her own dress collection.

In 1922, Oliver enrolled at the Slade School of Art to train as a portrait painter. It was his friend and mentor, Glyn Philpot, who directed him towards theatre design, much to the initial chagrin of Maud and Leonard (who would later become extremely proud of his achievements). In 1925, whilst preparing for his first exhibition – of theatrical masks made in papier mâché – at the Claridge Gallery in Brook Street, Oliver was introduced by the gallery's owners, Eva Mathias and Dr Archibald Propert, to Serge Diaghilev, founder of the Ballets Russes. Diaghilev commissioned some designs for his ballet, *Zéphyre et Flore*, to be shown at the Coliseum, London, the following year, and drawing on classical conventions, Oliver designed a set of gold 'Mycenean' masks, his first commission for the professional stage. It was well received.

From this point, Oliver's rise to fame was meteoric: immensely talented, witty and dashingly handsome, he was embraced by fashionable society, and his frequent companion was his beautiful and stylish sister, Anne. The two mixed in a social milieu within which fashion designers, artists, photographers, actors and musicians were gradually accorded a new celebrity status and were starting to be accepted socially by those with 'old' money. None the less, Anne's friendships with emerging London-based fashion designers Norman Hartnell and Charles James would have been considered entirely modern.

As a young unmarried woman Anne worked at Victoire, an exclusive dress shop in London's fashionable Sloane Street, where she learned to cut and sew to a highly professional standard. (Anne preserved a Victoire evening dress from the early 1930s, made in tomato-red silk with silver metal spangles around the neckline (Appendix 194).

Although wealthy both before and after marriage Anne – like Marion and Maud – possessed a very English frugal streak, coupled with a sense of achievement at making something from nothing. Anne was justly proud of her sewing skills, and into her personal albums she pasted press clippings such as this, which described how in her leisure she makes '… clothes as another woman might paint portraits or collect miniatures. I know no one smarter or more individual in her dress and the designing and making of these delectable garments is her great interest.'[7]

Plate 46 An evening dress belonging to Anne Messel, c.1924.

Fig. 30 Anne and Ronald Armstrong-
Jones on holiday, early 1930s.

Marriage

In 1925 Anne married Ronald Owen Lloyd Armstrong-Jones (1899–1966),
MBE QC DL, of Plas Dinas, Caernarvonshire. A friend of her brother
Linley, and the son of Margaret Elizabeth Roberts and Sir Robert
Armstrong-Jones, a distinguished doctor knighted for his services to
mental health, Ronald had been called to the Bar in 1922. Nicholson
portrays him as handsome, clever and rather serious:[8] like Anne, he loved
all country pursuits. The marriage took place on 22 July at the prestigious
gothic church of St Margaret's, Westminster, and was performed by the
Archbishop of Wales (Fig. 31). Anne had eight bridesmaids and three
child attendants, wearing cream chiffon dresses with headdresses and
girdles of green leaves that, as Nicholson points out, bore the stamp of
Oliver's creative genius.[9]

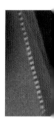

Fig. 31 Anne and Ronald Armstrong-
Jones's wedding, 1925.

Many other fashionable young brides in Anne's social circle chose a leading couturier to make their dresses. Anne's, however, appears to be homemade, possibly by her mother. It is a tabard-style garment with medieval overtones, made in cream silk satin with much hand-stitching (Plate 48). During the early 1920s pseudo-medieval-style wedding dresses, accentuated with loose, girdled belts and embellished with pearl embroidery, had been the height of fashion: this was the style chosen by Mary, the Princess Royal (1922), and by the Duchess of York (1923). However, by 1925 other fashionable young women such as Lady Alexandra (Baba) Curzon were married wearing ultra-modern knee-length *garçonne*-style dresses, featuring a long court train from the waist creating an interesting hybrid style. Anne's dress, like that worn by Princess Mary, was a longer romantic garment featuring pearl embroidery in a design of roses.[10]

Whilst Anne may have succumbed to royal influence, the medieval styling, embroidery and rose motifs are entirely in keeping with Maud's and Anne's personal predilections. Floral decoration (notably roses) and medieval styling – particularly expressed through a passion for long velvet capes – were to become amongst Anne's distinctive and enduring fashion signatures; and Maud grew old English roses at Nymans, which, at the time she was re-modelling along medieval lines. However, although the precise meanings of the embroidery on Anne's dress might be lost today, the design she chose reveals a passion for nature, history and narrative rather than impersonal, abstracted modernism – something the entire family carefully avoided.

Along with her wedding dress and shoes, Anne packed away an ivory satin drawstring bag embroidered in green, red and brown thread worked in a rose motif (Plate 47). This is typical of the work produced by Maud's Nymans Needlework Guild described in Chapter 4. It was a gift from Annie L. Wallace; her accompanying notes Anne characteristically preserved too. Marked 'July 19th Written at The Gables, Balcombe, Sussex', they read:

> Dear Miss Anne, Will you please accept the enclosed little bag with my best love and every good wish for the future. Yours sincerely Annie L. Wallace …
> As threads of gold compactly spun may years be blest to thee, memorandum for July 22nd 1925.

The wedding reception was held at Lancaster Gate. Following their marriage the couple lived at 25 Eaton Terrace, a gift from Maud and Leonard. Anne decorated the interior with furniture from the eighteenth century, a period which she and her brother, Oliver, adored for its style and its fashionable dress, and for its associations with Elizabeth Linley.

As well as the birth of her children – Susan Anne in 1927 and Antony Charles Robert in 1930 – the next few years saw Anne involved with helping Oliver. From 1926, Oliver started to design masks for the impresario C. B. Cochran's famous revues which comprised songs, sketches and chorus numbers. In 1929 Oliver was responsible for costuming five of the twenty-seven scenes in 'Wake Up and Dream', which was essentially a dancing revue. Anne worked with him to make the costumes for the ballerina Tilly Losch, who was dressed as a Manchu Marchioness for a sequence called 'China', for Alanova, who was dressed in eighteenth-century style dress, and for William Stephens, who wore a coolie costume.[11] With her own love of historical styling and the eighteenth century in particular, and the family's general preoccupation with China, these were costumes with which Anne had great affinity.

London fashion: 'Romantic "star dresses"'

By the early 1920s the London fashion industry – the formal court dressmakers of Queen Mary's generation – had begun to decline. A new generation of couture designers emerged who produced highly fashion-aware seasonal collections along the lines of the Parisian houses, albeit on a much smaller scale. However, it continued to be widely accepted that Paris designers were the originators of new trends. London designers had to face stiff competition, not only from across the Channel, but also on their own doorstep, as Worth, Chanel, Irfé and Schiaparelli – amongst others – opened London branches in the very same Mayfair streets. Anne, like her mother, was supremely confident in her own taste, and chose to patronise several London-based fashion talents.

One of the first of this new generation was Norman Hartnell, who opened his Bruton Street salon in 1923. With a penchant for full-skirted, embroidered and sequinned *robe-de-style* evening dresses, Hartnell was the natural couturier of choice for Anne. Oliver – possibly Anne too – first heard of Hartnell via Gladys Beattie Crozier. According to Oliver:

> 'Aunt' Gladys remained a constant visitor to Balcombe as well as to Nymans. She was basically a rather pre-Raphaelite beauty … I remember her excitement over a young artist who had been slaving away in a garret, making exquisite designs for the couture house Lucille [sic]. He turned out to be Norman Hartnell.[12]

Interviewed in 1985 on the occasion of the Norman Hartnell retrospective exhibition, Anne considered carefully his contribution to London couture, and on precisely why she wore his designs:

> I think he realized from the start the sort of romantic, yet suitable clothes that could complement the English beauty, and

Plate 47 Anne Armstrong-Jones's wedding bag, 1925.

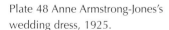

Plate 48 Anne Armstrong-Jones's wedding dress, 1925.

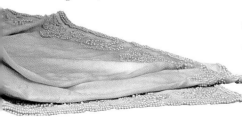

he developed a magic talent for making an English girl or woman look her best at all times and on all occasions, be it smart diplomatic soirée, the ballroom, or a race meeting, when, so often, the success of a sophisticated designer's lines depended on the wearer herself … As a humble dressmaker myself, I realise that the reason why he will always be on a pedestal lies in the perfection of his work, laced often with romantic 'star dresses' when needed … My own favourite clothes made by him, belonged to the era of chiffon and spotted net, and ruches.[13]

Anne may have owned several Hartnell dresses, but she chose to preserve the one with rose decoration from 1929. It is an arresting dress made in deep red silk chiffon, decorated with three-dimensional velvet roses and clusters of rosebuds (Plate 49 & Fig. 32).

Irfé

In 1927 Anne wore a striking white silk crêpe dress by the House of Irfé, with a black art-deco print depicting wheat and flowers (Plate 50). In *Beauty in Exile* Alexandre Vassiliev documents the history of Irfé in the context of the Russian émigrés who influenced the world of fashion.[14] Irfé was opened in Paris in 1924 by Prince Félix Youssoupoff and his wife Princess Irina.[15] Youssoupoff was a wealthy connoisseur of art, a collector of jewellery and a flamboyant socialite who adored dressing-up, but his notoriety arose from the fact that he claimed to be one of the assassins of Rasputin (confidant of Tsarina Alexandra) in 1916.[16] The current Lord Rosse recalled his parents taking him, during his childhood, to the exact spot of the murder in St Petersburg.[17]

Youssoupoff patronised the Stroganoff School of Applied Arts, a professional teaching institute set up with the assistance of Zemgor, an aid organisation for Russian refugees.[18] Some of the students were subsequently employed at Irfé, and may well have designed the print used on Anne's dress. The design also bears striking similarity to the art-deco woodblock textile prints that the Fauvist painter Raoul Dufy designed for the exclusive textiles company Bianchini-Férier in the early 1920s. By the time Anne purchased her dress, Irfé had opened a London branch.

In the context of the Messel Collection, this

opposite Plate 49 Dress belonging to Anne Armstrong-Jones by Norman Hartnell, 1929.

above Fig. 32 Anne Armstrong-Jones wearing Hartnell dress in *Vogue*, 1929.
Vogue / © The Condé Nast Publications Inc.

right Plate 50 Dress belonging to Anne Armstrong-Jones by Irfé, c.1927.

dress provides a rare example of fashionable couture adapted for maternity wear, and an insight into Anne's determination to seek out innovative design and remain elegant whilst pregnant.

The Messel Dress Collection also includes a green and pink fringed silk shawl with an art-deco-style floral print, from about 1925 (Appendix 277). It is not inconceivable that this might be linked to the Stroganoff school.

Floral fabrics and corsage: 'I *am* my garden'[19]

Throughout her life Anne retained her love of gardening, and flowers formed a core component of her fashion identity. Like Maud, Anne also customised her fashionable clothing – although to a lesser degree, as surviving pieces indicate – a practice that in the 1920s was still most unusual. Upon a green silk georgette afternoon dress, dating from the late 1920s, with a painterly printed design of waterlilies (Plate 51), Anne carefully applied tiny yellow glass beads into the centre of the flowers and metallic braid around the outlines of the leaves (Plate 52). Another very similar dress, with a handkerchief point hem, is made in yellow silk chiffon with a grey and black print of grasses and flowers (Appendix 165).

In 1931 Anne attended the Royal Enclosure at Ascot. She saved her ticket from this prestigious occasion in her album, and beside it pasted a cutting from the *Sketch* which notes that she wore '… a broderie anglaise frock with success and … a big rose in the very front of her bodice'.[20]

In 1933 press reports describe two other outfits with striking floral decorations: the first an evening dress of pale blue crêpe which the *Daily Express* noted had shoulder straps '… made of huge white feather flowers which unclipped can be worn as a necklace over the coat'.[21] Also placed in Anne's album is a press comment by Florence Roberts:

> Oliver Messel's sister the piquantly pretty Mrs Armstrong-Jones had on a lime green crêpe gown and a cape bordered with sable squirrel which tied under the left shoulder under a cluster of gigantic orchids worn to the first night of 'Mother of Pearl' at the Gaiety Exchange for which Oliver had designed the décor.[22]

As well as designing for the stage, Oliver was commissioned to design the scenery and costumes for many of the fashionable costume balls and charity pageants that were so popular during the 1920s and '30s, and this undoubtedly assisted the pair's movement through fashionable London society.

Evocations of the past: fancy dress and portraiture

Anne was astute and articulate in her fashion vocabulary, and her evocation of the past for her fancy dress and representation within portraiture was characteristically stylish and expedient. Dressed as the mythological beauty Ariadne for the Pageant of Great Lovers in May 1927, and accompanied by Oliver dressed as Bacchus (Fig. 33), Anne was singled out by the Duke of Kent as 'the best looking girl in the room' – a great compliment considering the Hollywood siren Tallulah Bankhead, dressed as Cleopatra, was also present.[23] Other historical figures portrayed by Anne – always set in the 1750–1820 period –

right Plate 51 Afternoon dress belonging to
Anne Armstrong-Jones, c.1929.

above Plate 52 Detail of dress, c.1929.

included Perdita Robinson, actress and mistress of the Prince Regent, at the Hyde Park Historical Pageant of 1928, again accompanied by Oliver dressed this time as Byron. She also played Lady Hamilton, Admiral Lord Nelson's radiant lover, at the Famous Beauties Ball of 1931.

Fancy dress afforded distinguished guests an opportunity to highlight their social status by dressing as famous relatives. Like Maud, Anne maximised the Messels' association with Elizabeth Linley by adopting styles and wearing original garments from the late eighteenth century. For the 1922 Devonshire House Ball, she wore the dress Maud had worn to the 1911 Chelsea Arts Ball dressed as Elizabeth Linley. Anne wore another eighteenth-century dress to several events, including the Pageant of Great Lovers (1927) and the charity matinée organised by Cathleen Mann, Marchioness of Queensbury (1897–1959), in 1931. She was accompanied to the matinée by her daughter Susan who, at four years old, wore a copy of her mother's dress (Fig. 35).

In her scrapbook is an undated cutting from the *Sketch* whose reporter described Anne wearing '... a gorgeous brocade gown which was worn

Fig. 33 Anne Armstrong-Jones and Oliver Messel dressed as Bacchus and Ariadne at the Pageant of Great Lovers Through the Ages, 6 May 1927

right Fig. 34 Painting of the Marchioness of Queensbury, Anne Armstrong-Jones, 1931, by Cathleen Mann.

Fig. 35 Anne Armstrong-Jones, with
her daughter Susan, wearing
eighteenth-century dress, 1931.

by one of her ancestors'. Research at Nymans shows it is highly likely that
this dress was in fact the eighteenth-century cream silk gown bought by
Maud and Leonard Messel from the Bath antiques dealer Rosa Dyer in
1924. Later in 1931 Anne invited the Marchioness, a fashionable artist, to
paint her portrait wearing the very same dress (Fig. 34).[24]

It has been remarked that Anne's portrait bears a distinct resemblance
(albeit in reverse) to a painting by Gainsborough, *Mrs. Sheridan*.[25] Anne,
who was twenty nine in the year the Mann portrait was commissioned,
would undoubtedly have been aware that Elizabeth Linley was twenty-
nine years old in 1783, the year of the Gainsborough painting.[26]

The following year, 1932, Anne again had her likeness made, this time
in a beguiling photographic portrait taken by Cecil Beaton at 'Biddesdon',
country home of Brian and Diana Guinness. She looks resplendent in a
panniered eighteenth-century style dress. Oliver, dressed as Paris, wears
one of his own creations designed for *Helen!* which opened that year
(Fig. 36). This portrait provided inspiration for a further two portraits of
Anne, one a chalk drawing by Oliver which remains within the family,

the other a painting by the little-known artist Harry Jonas, which was exhibited at The Royal Academy.

In striking contrast to these mannered portraits of Anne is a photograph that appeared on the cover of *The Field* in 1931 (Fig. 37) which shows her struggling to hold two salmon, one weighing 13lbs and the other 30lbs (both of which she had hooked with a prawn rod: the larger salmon was reported to be the heaviest caught on Crathie Water since the First World War).[27] It provides a rare glimpse of Anne (noted for wearing diamonds and looking immaculate even when gardening) in clothing that is entirely utilitarian.

Fig. 36 Cecil Beaton portrait of Anne Armstrong-Jones and Oliver Messel in fancy dress, 1932.

The vogue for neo-Victoriana

Whilst Anne 'dressed-up' in styles of the late eighteenth century, it was the late nineteenth century that was to provide inspiration for her fashionable evening wear. During the 1930s, couture fashion displayed influences from many sources, including neo-classicism, Victoriana, Surrealism, Hollywood costumes and Indo-Chinese clothing traditions. With her penchant for the romantic and picturesque, and her love of

right Fig. 37 Anne Armstrong-Jones on the cover of *The Field*, 1931.

history, materiality and dressing up, Anne championed the bustle-back Victorian style, and patronised those couturiers who excelled at this mode, adapting from dress history to suit modern life (pronounced bustles and crinolines were confined to evening dress).

Early signs of interest in Victoriana were evident in the predominantly homosexual, aesthetic coterie surrounding the writer, critic, art connoisseur and poet Harold Acton, who was a close friend of Anne. Acton recalled that at Oxford during the early 1920s:

> … I filled my rooms with Early Victorian objects, I bought a grey bowler hat, wore a stock and let my side-whiskas (sic) flourish ….
> I wore jackets with broad lapels and broad pleated trousers.[28]

Acton was at Oxford with Michael Rosse, Anne's second husband, while his friend Oliver Messel (they were both at Eton) was a student at the Slade in 1922. Acton describes Oliver travelling to Oxford from London to create decorations, based on scenes from Victorian history, for a fancy dress party.[29] Anne's contribution to this movement was less visible: throughout the 1920s and '30s she took responsibility for 18 Stafford Terrace whilst Roy was living there, ensuring that it was preserved almost as her grandparents had left it.

By the 1930s there was a more widespread interest in the Victorian period. Popular stage plays such as 'Victoria Regina', which in the Coronation Year, 1937, attracted massive audiences in New York, Paris and London, fed into and popularised this wave. So did numerous stage plays, and Hollywood films set in the Victorian period, such as *She Done Him Wrong* and *Little Women* (1933), and perhaps most famous of all – *Gone with the Wind* (1939). The latter starred Vivien Leigh, to whom Anne was compared in the diaries of novelist and biographer Evelyn Waugh and James Lees-Milne, diarist and National Trust activist. This was not a purist revival but rather involved a judicious mixing of styles both old and new.

As early as 1930 the press picked up on Anne's love of Victoriana. In 1930 the *Sunday Times* described Anne wearing a white tulle dress embroidered with blue flowers, a semi-crinoline and a blue chiffon shawl to the opera at Covent Garden.[30] In 1931 the *Daily Express* of 14 May reported 'Mrs Armstrong-Jones strolled in carrying a cluster of orchids in her hand and these emphasised the rather Victorian note of her outfit.' The same year the *Evening Standard* observed that 'Mrs Armstrong-Jones is so lucky to be able to wear both ancient and modern dress with equal success … she had a cream georgette dress with a bustle'.[31] In 1933, Anne's photograph appeared in *Harper's Bazaar* attending the Midnight Intimate Party of newly opened London couturier Victor Stiebel. She is seated with a group of friends including Nancy Mitford and Lady Oppenheimer. *Harper's* editorial remarked on her 'Victorian décolletage'.[32]

THE FIELD
THE COUNTRY NEWSPAPER
WITH WHICH IS INCORPORATED "LAND AND WATER"

VIII. No. 4113. SATURDAY, OCTOBER 24, 1931 POSTAGE {...}

A LADY ANGLER'S TWO DEE SALMON

Charles James: 'special dresses for special people'

Charles James's superlative designs, business history and mercurial personality were documented in depth in Elizabeth Ann Coleman's definitive catalogue *The Genius of Charles James*, which accompanied the exhibition she curated in 1982 at New York's Brooklyn Museum. Anne lent two of her own garments for the show: an evening coat from 1933 with short, kimono-like sleeves in aubergine silk faille (which is no longer in the collection), and her ribbon-bedecked, shell-pink ball gown from 1939 (Plate 71). The catalogue also reproduced the photograph of Susan wearing her mother's 'ribbon' dress in 1947 (Fig. 38). As such, this is a garment with fascinating multiple biographies. The catalogue references thirteen other James designs that Anne wore between 1933 and 1939. She wrote an insightful short article for the catalogue about James's London career. The focus of both the Brooklyn show and the exhibition publication was upon the couturier's American output in the period following the Second World War.

Coleman does not refer to the unique unlabelled pieces that Charles James made exclusively for Anne between 1935 and 1938, which she preserved in the family collection and lent to Brighton Museum.[33] These surviving garments, coupled with Anne and Oliver's memories, provide a new insight into James's early career in London.

Coleman reveals that, after working as a milliner and custom dressmaker in America between 1924 and 1929, he returned to London where in 1930 he opened premises at 1 Bruton Street, at first under the name of E. Haweis James.[34] Three years later he secured new premises in an elegant eighteenth-century house at 15 Bruton Street, which also became his residence. It was here that he hosted his Thursday afternoon salons for select clients and friends, including Cecil Beaton, Lady Ottoline Morrell, Virginia Woolf, Nancy Cunard and Stephen Tennant.

Anne could not recall precisely when she first met Charles James, but thought she was introduced to him by Baroness D'Erlanger.[35] They soon became great friends, with many shared interests including history and flowers.[36]

Coleman documents the earliest Charles James dress worn by Anne as the 'Spiral Wrap' or 'Taxi Street Dress', which James designed in 1929. Purchased in 1933, Anne's model was made from a textured weave black linen with a metal zip fastening that spun around the body (earlier versions had been closed with clasps). The dress has short sleeves, was bias-cut, and wrapped around the body one-and-a-half times.[37] (Appendix 167) By this date, Anne had become a fashionable society beauty whose portrait regularly appeared in the elite fashion press. A 1933 photograph by Cecil Beaton shows her wearing a late-afternoon or Ascot dress by Charles James in a pastel organza with short handkerchief drape sleeves and a trapezoidal bodice with a long flared skirt, accessorised with a floppy side-brimmed hat. Anne stands in front of a piece of scenery from

Fig. 38 Susan Armstrong-Jones wearing 'Ribbon dress' by Charles James in 1947.

Fig. 38 Cecil Beaton portrait of Anne Armstrong-Jones in Charles James Ascot outfit, 1933.

Plate 53 Detail of 'Ribbon dress', 1939.

Helen! (Fig. 38). The following year she was photographed by Peter Rose Pulham, swathed in spirals of pink and black tulle, in James's salon: the picture appeared in UK *Harper's Bazaar* in November 1934.

Although James's later designs imposed shape upon the female body, he was always highly selective about his clients (he frequently lacked funds, but he refused to dress those women he dismissed as 'frumps').[38] There was thus considerable kudos in being dressed by Charles James, and this of course was not lost on Anne. His bold designs required personality and style to wear, wealth to commission – and a back-up outfit if he failed to deliver on time! As Anne herself reflected, 'Charlie's creations then were specialities for special people – all masterpieces'.[39] Even in her thirties, Anne fitted James's ideal client specification by having the silhouette of an eighteen-year-old.[40] Nevertheless, when Anne had borne her children, she would have two ribs removed – which she insisted was for medical reasons, but which helped her maintain her slender silhouette and tiny waist into old age.[41]

Oliver wrote of his friend and colleague:

Charlie [James] was an extraordinary character, to say the least, and immediately bit the hand that fed him, insulted his most influential customers by telling them that their figures were lopsided and grotesque, or at a fitting he would cut through their underwear, leaving them naked, with their clothes in shreds.

His work, however, was so brilliant that a small group, including my darling sister and one or two others, determined to prop him up and try to help reorganise him. With buckets of soap and water we scrubbed his premises in Bruton Street while he constructed fabulous collections of dresses. The trouble was that the bailiffs were constantly at the door. There were never enough skilled hands available to help him stitch together the specially cut pieces ingeniously created by the master hand. As soon as Charlie cut his patterns and fitted them roughly for Anne, she would snatch them away, and being immensely talented with a needle, she would finish them off herself superbly at home.[42]

Separation, divorce and a fresh start

By the early 1930s Anne and Ronald's marriage was floundering. Nicholson records Ronald as being

> … very ambitious; his work kept him busy and he soon grew tired of the endless round of parties, the dressing up and all the theatrical gossip which his wife enjoyed so much. Anne determined to do as she pleased and the couple ceased to go everywhere together. In 1933 they agreed to have a trial separation.[43]

Anne soon began to spend time with Michael, 6th Earl of Rosse, with whom she was to enter a passionate and enduring love affair. Michael, who had known Oliver since his teenage years, was descended from an Anglo-Irish family with a vast gothick castle at Birr, County Offaly. Anne's marriage ended in divorce on 28 August, 1935, and three weeks later she and Michael were married.

Conclusion

Many women in Anne's situation – wealthy and about to embark upon a new life – might well have discarded their old clothing, especially their first wedding dress. Furthermore, as fashions had changed so much by 1935, her garments from the 1920s and early '30s would have been thought démodé and generally unwearable by 1935. But Anne was a natural collector whose clothing was intensely personal. Like her mother before her, she was also acutely aware that memories can be drawn and histories constructed from deep within the fabric of our clothes.

I am very grateful to Eleanor Thompson for information on Anne's fancy dress.

[1] *Evening News*, 1 February 1931.

[2] Charles Castle, *Oliver Messel: A Biography*, Thames & Hudson, London, 1986, p. 25.

[3] Anne, Countess of Rosse, 'The Eccentric Upbringing of a Collectors Daughter', unpublished document, early 1980s, Nymans Archive, A/33/2.

[4] Ibid., p. 20.

[5] Ibid., p. 19.

[6] Shirley Nicholson, *Nymans: the story of a Sussex garden*, Sutton Publishing, in association with the National Trust, Gloucestershire, 2001, p. 71.

[7] *Evening News*, 1 February 1931.

[8] Shirley Nicholson, p. 73.

[9] Ibid.

[10] I am grateful to Caroline Windsor for her research on Anne's dress.

[11] Roger Pinkham (ed.), *Oliver Messel*, V&A, London, 1983, p. 77.

[12] Charles Castle, *Oliver Messel*, p. 30.

[13] Exhibition Catalogue, *Norman Hartnell 1901–1979*, The Royal Pavilion, Art Gallery and Museums, Brighton, 1985.

[14] Alexandre Vassiliev, *Beauty in Exile,* Harry N. Abrams, New York, 1998, pp. 265–83.

[15] Irfé derives from the first two letters of each of their names.

[16] In 2004 a new theory emerged – that it was British agent Oswald Rayner who killed Rasputin. *Sunday Telegraph*, 19 September 2004.

[17] Interview Lou Taylor and Eleanor Thompson, Brighton, 2004.

[18] H. Menegaldo, *Les Russes à Paris*, Autrement, Paris, Coll. Monde, no. 110. October 1998, p. 119 in Valerie Guillaume, *Souvenir Moscovites* 1869–1930, Paris Musee, 2000, p. 84.

[19] *Woman's Weekly*, 7 September 1985, p. 4.

[20] *Sketch*, 24 June 1931.

[21] *Daily Express,* 13 April 1933.

[22] Florence Roberts, unattributed newspaper article, 4 February 1933.

[23] *Vogue*, 7 May 1927.

[24] The portrait was exhibited at the Royal Society of Portrait Painters, but its current location is unknown.

[25] The National Gallery Washington, Mellon Collection.

[26] I am grateful to Caroline Windsor for making this connection.

[27] *The Field*, 24 October 1931.

[28] Harold Acton, *Memoirs of an Aesthete*, Hamish Hamilton, London, 1948: 118–19.

[29] Ibid., p. 124.

[30] *Sunday Times*, 23 June 1930.

[31] *Evening Standard*, 7 December 1931.

[32] *Harper's Bazaar*, 10 June 1933.

[33] See Chapter 7 and the Conclusion for details of these pieces.

[34] Elizabeth Anne Coleman, *The Genius of Charles James*, The Brooklyn Museum, New York, 1982, pp. 78–79.

[35] Ibid., p. 111.

[36] Ibid., p. 8.

[37] Ibid., p. 128.

[38] Ibid., p. 112.

[39] Ibid., p. 111.

[40] Ibid., p. 91.

[41] Interview with Lady Alicia Parsons, Birr, 27 June 2004.

[42] Charles Castle, *Oliver Messel,* pp. 97–98.

[43] Shirley Nicholson, *Nymans*, p. 89.

CHAPTER SIX

The Rosse family in Ireland

The heritage of Birr Castle Demesne and Anne's patronage of Irish fashion[1]

Elizabeth McCrum and Lou Taylor

The Irish connection in our story first appears in the friendship between Leonard Messel and the Irish connoisseur Hugh Lane. Typically of Leonard Messel, who treasured his contacts with many of the great connoisseurs of his period, this friendship was so close that Leonard and Maud went furniture and antique hunting in Ireland with Lane. Lane was one of London's, as well as Dublin's, great collectors and a famous dealer in old master paintings. He owned work by Titian, Goya, Lancret and Greuze and in 1904 he organised the first, major exhibition of Irish Art at the Guildhall.[2] Lane was also a pioneering collector of French Impressionism and paintings for his Dublin Gallery, which included *La Musique aux Tuileries* by Manet, *Sur la Plage* by Degas, *Les Parapluies* by Renoir and *La Cheminée* by Vuillard.

In 1909 Lane bought Lindsey House, 100 Cheyne Walk, Chelsea, built in 1675 and described by Thomas Bodkin as full of treasures. These included 'pictures, statuary, bronzes, ceramics, and furniture.' Lane, he adds, 'gave simple dinners to his friends before showing them his latest acquisitions.'[3] Lane's influence on interior design before the First World War was considerable. Anne, Countess of Rosse wrote that her parents' home, at Lancaster Gate, as discussed earlier, 'was a collector's house very much in the mould of the great collector and advisor to collectors, Hugh Lane. It was full of wonderful oriental art and marvellous Spanish and Italian furniture.'[4] Lane was appointed Director of the National Gallery of Ireland. In 1915 on a journey to New York he was drowned

Detail of dress by Irene Gilbert, 1948. *See Plate 58*

112

when the *Lusitania* was torpedoed. His body was never recovered and neither were the crates of paintings by Monet, Rembrandt, Rubens and Titian that were travelling with him. His will was bitterly contested between Dublin and London for fifty years, over possession of his contemporary continental paintings, a situation that was ameliorated, but not resolved, through an agreement made in the 1950s to rotate the pictures.[5]

Ireland

The family connection with Ireland was revived in 1935, when Anne Armstrong-Jones married Michael, the 6th Earl of Rosse. His family name was Parsons and Anne had known him for many years. Thus the Irish connection to the Parsons' crenellated, Gothick Birr Castle, was established.

Michael was descended from the thirteen generations of the Anglo-Irish Parsons family, who settled on the Birr plantation in County Offaly (former King's County), seventy miles outside Dublin, in the early seventeenth century. Oisin Deery writes that the Parsons were 'members of the elite Protestant ascendancy in Birr.' The site of Birr Castle has an ancient history. A well related to St Brendan, who founded a monastery there in 549 AD, can still be found in the castle grounds. By the tenth century the Gaelic chieftains of the O'Carrol family had established ownership of the area and built the 'Black Castle' on land nearby. By 1619, the plantation of the O'Carrols 'by settlers from England' was underway and on 22 June, 1620, the castle passed into the hands of Mr Lawrence Parsons, brother of Sir William Parsons, Surveyor General of Ireland.[6]

Against a background of centuries of colonial rule of Ireland from Westminster and the consequent political and military unrest dating back to the Anglo-Norman invasion of Ireland in the twelfth century, and direct government rule by English Viceroys and Anglo-Irish officials from the period of King Henry VIII, the Parsons were a remarkable and unusual Anglo-Irish aristocratic family. Their intellectual and creative talents emerged through both arts and sciences. In the 1790s, Sir Laurence Parsons became a friend and supporter of Theobald Wolfe Tone, the radical Irish advocate of parliamentary reform, Irish independence and Catholic emancipation. Laurence Parsons was a MP for Trinity College from 1782–90 and for Kings County (Offaly) from 1791–1807. In 1800, he voted against the Act of Union, which dissolved the Irish Parliament in favour of direct rule from Westminster. Deery writes that he retired from politics soon after and became Joint Postmaster General, responsible for the development of the famous post office building in Dublin. In 1807 Laurence Parsons inherited the title of Earl of Rosse from an uncle, becoming the 2nd Earl. In 1836 his son William married Mary Field, from a Yorkshire family. The pair 'were immediately invited to occupy Birr

Plate 54 'The Leviathan' telescope, Birr Castle Demense, constructed 1842–45.

Castle by the 2nd Earl, who was then in ailing health and who had decided to move to Brighton.[7] He died in 1841.

William, the 3rd Earl of Rosse, famously became an internationally recognised astronomer. He designed and built the largest telescope in the world, nicknamed the *Leviathan,* a vast construction in full view of the great windows of Birr Castle (Plate 54). For almost seventy years this remained the world's largest telescope. The Earl observed for the first time the nebula – Messier 51 – in the constellation of Canes Venatici, as well as the spiral nature of some of the galaxies and was named a Member of the Board of Visitors to the Greenwich Observatory.[8] He and his wife, Mary, had eleven children of whom only four boys survived. In the 1854–65 period, Mary became a highly accomplished, pioneer photographer. Her darkroom survives at Birr, as well as a series of group and portrait shots of her family and friends, 'naturally and spontaneously arranged'.[9]

One of their surviving sons, Sir Charles Parsons, became a pioneering engineer, patenting his new steam turbine engine in 1884 and placing the first turbine engine in a ship, the *Turbinia,* in 1897. On 5 January, 2005, the Science Museum, London, in a press release about the refurbishment of its Energy Gallery, stated that Parsons was one of the 'luminaries' whose work was to be highlighted and that his 'steam turbine [is] still used in most power stations.'[10] The family also has a continuing and impressive record in public service related to the arts, museums and to the conservation of British and Irish architectural heritage, particularly of the Georgian period. It was this ancient and erudite family that Anne Armstrong-Jones, daughter of Maud and Leonard Messel, joined in 1935.

Birr Castle

Paul Caffrey writes: 'If there is such a thing as Irish style, it is essentially a country house one, and it is in the rural parts of Ireland that survivals of the unique characteristics of interior design may be found both in the vernacular interiors of the country cottage or farmhouse and in the great country houses.' Caffrey, writing of the heritage of country-house architecture after 1700, adds that this included influences from Holland, English classical architecture, Rococo chinoiserie and neo-classicism in the late eighteenth century. The latter is evidenced, for example, by James Wyatt's designs at Castle Coole, County Fermanagh, dating from the 1790s and the intact interiors from the 1820s at Newbridge House, County Dublin and at Killadoon in County Kildare. The Gothic Revival style of the early to mid-nineteenth century, as Caffrey notes, found its place, too, in Irish country-house architecture, seen in the interiors of Lismore Castle, County Waterford, designed by A. W. N. Pugin, and at Humewood, County Wicklow, designed by William White and which still today 'contains the most virtuoso Gothic Revival interiors surviving in Ireland.'[11]

Deery explains that this same Gothick was the style also favoured by the 2nd Earl of Rosse, Laurence Parsons. Starting from 1807, he reoriented the castle 'by turning the old building around in order to have it face the park, as well as heightening and crenallating the structure in fashionable Gothic style' (Plate 55). The great vaulted Gothick drawing-room was added in about 1818, with its large matching arched windows overlooking the grounds. In 1836, when the 3rd Earl and Mary, Countess of Rosse took over the castle, the Countess designed and had made the prettiest, wooden, Gothick bedroom suite, with cupboard and tester bed, with swirled white and gold painted edging. Lord Rosse confirms that an 'additional ribbed head [was] added to the bed to the design of Lord Snowdon when he was a child, made by Willy Eades, the estate carpenter.'[12]

The impressive, crenulated entrance gates and the great stables of the castle were added later. They were designed by Mary, the 3rd Countess, in consultation with her uncle, Richard Wharton Myddleton. The construction of these additions was part of the philanthropic relief work provided when the effects of the potato famine were at their worst in Birr. By the end of the famine over 15,000 people had died in County Offaly and 20,000 more had emigrated.[13] Memories of the behaviour of Anglo-Irish landowners during the famine are stamped on Irish history and it is of interest here to note that in 1999, when he opened the new Birr Castle Historic Science Centre, Noel Treacy, the Irish Minister for Science, Technology and Commerce carefully referred to the 'unique and outstanding contribution' made by the Earls of Rosse, 'to Ireland, in dark and difficult days. … It is well known that the Earls of Rosse were exceedingly generous and fair, to the local people, during this terrible time, in Ireland.'[14] The 3rd Countess designed the metalwork on new keep gates installed at this time, which still give access to the castle, casting the bronze sections herself.[15] No women's clothes from this long family history survive.

Plate 55 Birr Castle.

The gardens at Birr

The oldest surviving tree in the grounds of Birr Castle is a much cared for *Quercus robur*, with a girth of 6.5 metres, standing in the middle of the wild meadow where the swifts swoop in the summer. It is believed to be over 600 years old and is named 'the Carol Oak', after the O'Caroll family. The grounds at Birr were first landscaped in the 1740.[16] In 1826, a delicate little suspension bridge (one of the earliest known in the world) was built just below the castle windows.[17] By the mid-Victorian period, a rocky fernery had been added and the family interest in rare trees and plants was firmly established. A *Cypressus macrocarpa*, similar to a

Monterey pine, was planted at Birr in about 1855 and flourishes today. Interestingly, well before the Messel and Rosse families became so closely intertwined, a *magnolia delavayi*, from South China, was bought in 1912 and planted only a decade or so after this tree had been introduced into the British Isles.[18] Today the river Camcor runs through the estate, sluicing over a waterfall. The river was diverted here in 1880 by the 4th Earl, in order to generate hydro-electric power for the castle and the town. The ruined generator still stands in the grounds. His son, the 5th Earl, notes Nicholson, supported key botanical expeditions to China before 1914[19] as had Leonard Messel at the same time (Plate 56).

Michael, the 6th Earl, inherited his title at the age of twelve when his father, serving with the Irish Guards, was killed in the First World War. From the 1930s Lord Rosse held distinguished positions in many key education and arts organisations both in Ireland and in England. He and Anne shared many passionate commitments, particularly for the conservation of Georgian architectural heritage and became key figures in the establishment of the Georgian Group in the late 1930s. Michael was on the Council of the National Trust from 1946, chairperson of the Standing Commission on Museums and Galleries (1956–78), President of the Friends of the National Collections of Ireland and of the Royal Horticultural Society of Ireland (1959–69), a member of the Arts Council of Ireland (1953–74) and of the Advisory Council of the V&A and the Science Museum, London. He was pro-chancellor of University College Dublin from 1965 (Vice-Chancellor, 1949–65) during which period fund-raising visits were made on behalf of the University to the United States.

Plate 56 Birr gardens.

Birr in the 1930s

By the time of Michael's marriage to Anne Armstrong-Jones, Birr Castle Demesne had become run down and required energetic refurbishment. Thus from the moment of her second marriage in 1935, Lady Rosse threw herself with her usual energy and creative spirit into successfully reviving the decoration of Birr Castle and its great gardens. Caffrey notes that she 'reinterpreted some of the most beautiful Victorian rooms in Ireland in the skilful arrangement of furniture, flowers and pictures (Fig. 39). The ballroom is hung with Victorian green and gold damask patterned wallpaper and during the 1940s, Lady Rosse hung red flock wall paper in the dining room and restored the dado.'[20] She also found Mary, Countess of Rosse's Gothick bedroom furniture in a badly dilapidated condition, famously rescuing it and embroidering new hangings for the tester bed herself, which remain in place today.

Birr Castle Demesne Gardens

Anne and Michael's marriage thus became a marriage of two great gardens. Trees and shrubs were transferred from Nymans to Birr with much success, including the famous rhododendrons, *eucryphia nymansay*. Michael became a specialised dendrologist, whilst Anne turned the kitchen garden at Birr castle into a beautiful formal garden from a seventeenth-century design. The Rosses continued Leonard's commitment to discovering and raising rare trees and plants. Anne and Michael Rosse spent part of their honeymoon in China. Deery confirms that whilst in Peking, they met Professor H. H. Hu, a botanist and the Director of the Fan Memorial Institute of Biology.

Plate 57 'Anne Rosse' peony.

A group of hybrids were raised at Birr, including the famous *Paeonia ludlowii-hybrid* 'Anne Rosse'. This is a pollinated cross between a tree peony discovered in 1936 in the Tsangpo Gorge in South East Tibet, with another discovered on one of the Chinese expeditions in 1937, sponsored by Michael. This astonishing flower has four-inch, lemon-yellow flowers streaked with red, and won an award of merit from the Royal Horticultural Society in 1961.[22] (Plate 57)

Anne's commitment to Birr Castle Demesne was total. Nicholson writes that it was Lady Rosse 'who was primarily responsible for the new gardens which were taking shape in Birr' and that 'her drawings and notes for the planting schemes have been preserved'. Nicholson adds that Maud and Leonard Messel happily visited Birr Castle many times, that seeds and plants were exchanged between the two family gardens and that the Head Gardner at Nymans, James Comber, also visited Birr, as of course did Anne's brother, Oliver Messel and the rest of this large extended family.[23]

Anne, 6th Countess of Rosse and her support for Irish fashion

Once she had a base in Ireland and began to spend time there, Anne
Rosse sought out the fashion designers of her new home. The Countess's
taste in fashion was, as we have seen in Chapter 5, sophisticated and
cosmopolitan, but she never had the metropolitan disdain for the
provincial. Throughout her life she saw design with a clear, fresh and
unprejudiced eye. This attitude made her an invaluable patron of the
emerging Irish fashion industry

Given the economic malaise of Ireland in the mid-twentieth century,
the development of a home grown fashion industry, let alone a successful
one which won international esteem, was something of a phenomenon.
Years of protectionism had led to uncompetitive and old-fashioned
business practices, there was low growth and little investment in industry,
and unemployment and emigration levels were high. There had been
successful Anglo-Irish designers such as Edward Molyneux, John
Cavanagh and Digby Morton, but they had spent their careers in Paris or
London. A series of factors combined to produce a surprisingly

Fig. 39 Portrait of Anne, Countess of
Rosse in Birr Castle by Snowdon,
c.1950.

advantageous springboard for the new fashion trade centred in Dublin. The receipt of Marshall Aid meant that the government had to rethink its economic planning. The Industrial Development Company, the Undeveloped Areas Act, and Coras Tráchtála – also known as CTT or the Dollar Board – were set up, all three of which aided the textile and clothing industry. CTT, with its remit to help companies advance export business and produce the right products, was the most crucial since it concentrated on the American market, vital for the success of the fashion industry in the 1950s.

The distinctive fabrics of Ireland – the tweeds, linens, knitwear, crochet and lace – were a source of inspiration to Irish fashion designers and were an obvious advantage in the American market, where their nostalgic and sentimental associations proved a selling point. Importantly, they were also in line with the preferred fabrics sought by international fashion. By the 1950s, international fashion was looking for original and unusual fabrics for both the highly tailored daywear and the romantic evening styles of the time. Irish fabrics, as modified and refined by the demands of local designers, were admired and used in mainstream fashion.

This new generation of Irish designers was the last crucial element in the inception of the Irish fashion industry. Through a mixture of creative and marketing skills they raised the profile of their trade to the point when, in March 1956, *Harper's Bazaar* had on its cover 'Spring Collections Paris London Dublin Italy'.

Anne Rosse's connection with Irish designers began with her patronage of Irene Gilbert, the fashion designer who remained most closely associated with her. Gilbert was a traditionally perfectionist couturière, who designed, as Madeleine Vionnet did, directly on a stand. She was born in Thurles, County Tipperary, to an Irish father and a Yorkshire mother, probably around 1910. Throughout her life she disliked self-publicity, and it is quite hard to discover basic facts such as her birth date. She worked in Dublin in her late teens, then went to London to train with a court dressmaker for about five years. She married in 1935, and worked for British intelligence during the Second World War. In the mid-40s, her marriage over, she returned to Dublin, and opened a millinery and clothes shop in South Frederick Street in 1947. At a fashion show in Jammet's restaurant, she included some garments of her own design, and following success with these, opened her salon in 1951, after which she showed her own collections every season. In 1954, CTT sent her to the United States, with a collection which 'resulted in excellent press'[24] and led to media coverage in the British newspapers. Subsequently she showed collections in London from 1955. Other work included costume design for films,[25] and the 1957 design of the Aer Lingus uniform. Growing international and national success led to her moving into premises on St Stephen's Green in 1960. She retired in 1968, at a time when many couturiers felt themselves overtaken by new demands for casual, cheap, youthful styles, which were the antithesis of made-to-measure standards.

Irene Gilbert's tailoring skills were best represented in daywear, in which, too, her distinctive use of Irish tweeds was seen. In common with her fellow designers, she worked with woollen mills to make them refine their products and produce light tweeds for dress wear. She was associated with Avoca Handweavers, among others, and famously sent the Misses Wynn of Avoca a dried hydrangea head to help them produce the right colour for her admired hydrangea-coloured tweeds of 1955. She also worked with McNutts of Donegal, demanding and getting the exact short lengths she required. [26]

In evening wear, Gilbert's handmade Irish lace dresses, and, in the 1960s, her draped dresses were much admired. However, the variety of her evening styles went far beyond this, as evidenced by the Countess's collection. The two women became friends, and Anne was to write a most affectionate obituary of Irene Gilbert in 1985.[27] She described her as one of the greatest of Dublin's many mid-twentieth century geniuses, and wrote that she herself had been 'one of the earliest to recognise the magic quality of her exquisite and original designs.' She continued:

> When I first came to Ireland, there was the myth that ladies of fashion had to resort to the salons of Paris or London to be really well dressed, and that Dublin could produce only dull tweedy suits or dowdy dresses for race meetings or home wear … I too then sought the luxury of Paris or London clothes … She used unusual materials – Donegal tweed specially made for her in rare colours, Limerick lace still made, Irish crochet or fabulous French silks. Her cut and finish were superb often completed with her own hands. Her creations were essentially sophisticated, enormously imaginative and romantic.

Respect was mutual between the two women – Irene Gilbert, or 'Gilly', as the Countess called her, stated in a 1963 interview that of all her clients, the Countess of Rosse had the best imagination for clothes. 'She is never slow to disagree with me, but I always welcome it because she is a woman of exceptional talent with a needle. When I make something for her, it combines the best of our ideas.'[28]

This collaborative experience meant that there is a recognisable Rosse's style in Gilbert's clothes for the Countess. Most were fitted to show off her size-10 figure, and most were in strong colours often combined with black. The decorative elements were often unusual, but effective and restrained. The first surviving Gilbert dress at Birr is the scarlet taffeta ball gown of 1948 (Plate 58), which according to her maid, Margaret Shortt, was made to show off her rubies. Three black 1950s full-length evening dresses, one of lace, one of velvet devoré stripes in complex cut, and one trimmed with blue daisies, also conform to her

Fig. 40 Robert Graham portrait of the Queen Mother with the Countess of Rosse wearing a Sybil Connolly design, mid-1950s.

style, as do two outfits from the 1960s (Appendix 211, 215 & 216). The first is an empire line evening dress with a strong shoulder line created by scallops of cream satin below black satin (Appendix 223), and the second a cocktail outfit, a purple satin coat with a dress of purple satin overlaid with black roundels (Plate 59). An evening coat of black wool and velvet, the fabrics separated by a diagonal seam, and an empire line evening dress, with beaded bodice are other late Gilbert pieces. Later in life, Anne also wore quite bright colours such as the lime green satin Gilbert evening dress (Appendix 222).

Another colour palette can be seen in the early 1950s brown and gold brocade evening dress (Appendix 209), in which the Countess is photographed with the Queen Mother and her husband at Buckingham Palace (Fig. 40) and in another dress, which has a note pinned to it 'The last one Gilly ever made me', of 1969, the year after Gilbert retired. This is of dark beige embroidered silk, a sleeveless sheath which she wore when she was sixty seven, with matching coat (Appendix 224). A pale olive green satin coat with patterned dress of fine cut shows the self covered buttons favoured by the Countess as well as the faint pin holes left by her diamond pins (Appendix 208). The two surviving examples of Gilbert's daywear tailoring for the Countess are a green tweed suit, with coat, jacket and skirt (the skirt is now missing) and a tan tweed coat, cleverly cut at the stand-up neckline (Appendix 185–86).

There are three dresses at Birr by Sybil Connolly, who did more than any other designer to give Irish fashion an international reputation. Like Gilbert, she was half Irish and trained in London (in her case at the court dressmaker, Bradleys), before coming to Ireland after the Second World War. Connolly was employed by Jack Clarke, whose coat and suit factory

left Plate 58 A ball gown by Irene Gilbert belonging to Anne, Countess of Rosse, 1948.

above Plate 59 Cocktail outfit by Irene Gilbert, c.1968.

traded under the name of 'Country Wear' and who had begun to export to North America in 1947. She was initially the manager of his retail outlet 'Richard Alan', but had ambitions to establish a couture section in this ready-to-wear business. After the first couture designer left in 1952, she took his role, and used her own name for the couture line. A 1953 trip to the United States on a storm-tossed *Queen Elizabeth* was the first of many trips to America in which Miss Connolly's charm and PR skills, added to her admired designs, paved the way for both her and other Irish designers' success in America. Later she showed her collections equally successfully in Australia. In 1957 she set up her own fashion house in Dublin's Merrion Square, which was her home, showroom and workroom until her death in 1998. She used a wide variety of Irish fabrics such as Irish poplin and dyed Carrickmacross lace, but is best known for her pleated linen dresses. These required nine yards of fine handkerchief linen to produce one yard of a finely pleated fabric which was virtually crease-proof. Dyed in subtle or bright colours, the dresses were very flattering and became design classics. The pleated linen dress at Birr, probably of the mid-1950s, worn by Susan Armstrong-Jones, is a particularly good example. It is a full-skirted, white-pleated linen evening dress, with the pleats swagged, and with a fitted, low necked, sleeveless bodice (Appendix 278). A late 1950s silk ball gown, with a floral pattern of soft brown, a colour popular at that date, showing the strong outline often seen in Connolly's evening dresses, and a 1960 'Mermaid' evening dress of cream and gold lace comprise the other Sybil Connolly outfits at Birr (Appendix 214 & 219).

Sybil Connolly, like Irene Gilbert, sourced and commissioned fine and feature tweeds for outfits such as her famous 1952 'Irish Washerwoman' outfit, an evening ensemble whose long skirt was made of the red flannel seen in the petticoats worn as traditional dress on the western seaboard of Ireland. The Countess, however, seems not to have patronised the tweeds of Irish designers, but preferred to work with Dublin tailoring firms. Many of these tailored tweed very skilfully, and exported equally successfully. While operating at a level below couture, they have consistently contributed to the reputation of Irish fabric and fashion. When Anne saw wool drying on sea rocks in Connemara, in the West of Ireland, she had it dyed red, and made into a suit, probably of her own design, by S&M Jacobs, of 20 Dawson Street, in Dublin. It was worn for shooting, with red stockings and boots.[29] (Appendix 182) This firm made at least four other suits for her and her daughter, Lady de Vesci, in a variety of

Plate 60 Coat by Irene Gilbert, 1950s.

coloured tweeds – bright blue, lavender, brown and green. Most have self-covered buttons and printed silk linings, probably matched to a blouse (Appendix 183–85).

The Countess was faithful to 'Gilly', and felt some unease about favouring other designers. Apart from Sybil Connolly, whom she patronised to a limited degree, she did not appear to acquire the work of other successful Irish contemporary designers such as Neilli Mulcahy, Mary O'Donnell, Clodagh or Pat Crowley, who had worked for Gilbert for seven years. The present Countess of Rosse owns a fine Irish crochet mini coat-dress, by Mary O'Donnell, dating from the late 1960s (Appendix 281). These designers enjoyed great success in the United States as well as at home, and were known for their use of Irish fabrics and embellishments. Gilbert was without doubt the most skilled and inventive couturier of her generation – the others had different strengths, which did not conform to the Countess's taste. Later in the 1960s, and mostly after the retirement of Irene Gilbert, she did use and admire the work of two Irish based designers. They both came to Ireland from abroad, but had made their homes there for many years.

Ib Jorgensen came to Ireland with his family from his native Denmark in 1949. He studied dress design at the Grafton Academy in Dublin, which has produced many successful designers. He then worked for Nicholas O'Dwyer's clothing company, which employed an elderly workforce of excellent tailors who left their mark on Jorgensen's work. His tailoring and finishing, like Irene Gilbert's, has always been of the highest standard. Ib opened his own house in 1958, and his success grew until in the 1970s he had a splendid showroom and workroom in Fitzwilliam Square, a boutique in Dawson Street and a shop in Bond Street, London. His first wife, Patricia Jorgensen, produced the printed, hand-painted and embroidered designs that were another hallmark of the house. When the Countess first contacted Ib about buying his work, she asked him 'Do you think Gilly will mind?', to which Ib could only reply that he didn't think she would be too pleased.[30]

For Anne Rosse, Ib designed a variety of outfits, which reflected prevailing fashions, and, perhaps, some indication that she was trying out different styles as she grew older. A mushroom silk crêpe wrap day dress contrasted with a 'Laura Ashley'-type sprigged black cotton voile long dress with long sleeves, and high ruffled high neck. He also made a sharp outfit of a green silk organza shift dress and matching coat, the dress with beaded stripes, and a classically beautiful black silk crêpe empire-line evening dress with a very deep cowl neck (Appendix 174–75, 230–31).

The second foreign-born designer patronised by the Countess towards the end of her life was another master tailor. Thomas Wolfangel hailed from Stuttgart in Germany, and came to Ireland in 1957. He worked in Sligo before going to Dublin where he first worked for the designer Kat Petersen, then opened his own business in the mid-1960s. His preference for sharp, bright colours, his tailoring skills, best seen in his suits and coats, and his characteristic embellishments such as pin tucking and sleeve detail concurred with what we know of Anne's own tastes. The number of Wolfangel outfits in Birr are second only to the Gilbert outfits. Again, a friendship grew between the designer and the client. Mr Wolfangel speaks with great affection of the countess. His Georgian premises in Baggot Street were chilly and Lord Rosse would always phone before on the morning of her visit to ensure that they were warmed. She was, he says, the kindest lady, representative of the 'old world' at its best. They sat together and sketched. The Countess looked for a classic style, which flattered her figure, and enjoyed bright colours – this despite the fact that the first garment she bought was a brown coat. She wandered into his shop and tried on a coat, which had been returned for alteration. It fitted her perfectly, she kept it, and from then on her patronage, as he was starting off his business, was invaluable. She always bought something new for the Chelsea Flower Show.

There are two Wolfangel double-breasted evening coats at Birr, one of a black, gold and cream print, and one of black velvet with frogging and duffle buttons (Appendix 241–42). A day suit of emerald wool also has black frogging as a front edge trim (Appendix 188). Two day coats reveal the confluence of the Countess's and Wolfangel's taste. A bright blue wool coat with a pin-tucked yoke, strong shaping on the sleeve head, black velvet trim to collar and cuff and self covered buttons is a particularly good example (Appendix 189). Another navy coat of complex but effective cut, which has a matching print dress, is the equal of Irene Gilbert's best work. Two exuberant evening dresses also survive. One is of a bright red, green and black printed silk, with a floating back panel, and the other is of satin – on one side of a diagonal seam, the left side and sleeve of the bodice are cream, while the rest of the dress is purple. (Appendix 220–21). The seaming echoes that of the Irene Gilbert black coat also at Birr, and further indicates the consistency of the Countess's taste. Many of these clothes were exhibited at the Ulster Museum in 1997.[31]

The Countess of Rosse, as she made clear in an interview, did not patronise Irish designers just because they were Irish. On official trips with her husband, for example when as Chancellor of Dublin University he visited the United States, she did appear to wear the work of her adopted country's designers as a matter of policy. Otherwise, they were patronised on their own merits, and as they conformed in skills and creativity to her own firm tastes. She only seems to have worn Irish fabrics as daywear, and enjoyed the new bright, light tweeds, which were being produced by Irish mills in response to the new demands of fashion. She did not, however, wear the Irish laces, crochets or linens, which were so internationally successful at the time. For example, only atypical and non-Irish designs by Sybil Connolly were worn by her.

Anne Rosse was loyal to her favoured designers, particularly to Irene Gilbert, who remains closely associated with her and to whom she was her ideal client. Just as the Countess had the confidence to wear her own designs at the highest social events, she happily wore Irish designs on the most prominent occasions, as attested by the Irene Gilbert dress, which she wore to Buckingham Palace. She knew and appreciated excellence in fashion design wherever she found it, and by her own admission, was surprised and pleased to have found it in Ireland.

[1] With thanks to Dr. Paul Caffrey, National College of Art and Design, Dublin, for his advice on first half of this chapter.

[2] Jorgensen Fine Art Gallery, Dublin, exhibition catalogue, 2004.

[3] Thomas Bodkin, *Hugh Lane and His Pictures*, Pegasus press for the Irish Free State Press, 1932, pp. 25–27.

[4] Charles Castle, *Oliver Messel, a Biography*, Thames and Hudson, London, 1986, p. 49

[5] Anne Kelly, 'The Lane bequest, A British-Irish cultural conflict revisited', *Journal of the History of Collections,* vol. 16, no 1. 2004. pp. 89–110.

[6] Oisin Deery, *A Compact History of Birr*, Tama Books, Dublin, 2001, pp. 13, 17.

[7] Ibid., pp. 46–47, 60.

[8] Ibid., pp. 62–63.

[9] Ibid., p. 68.

[10] A vast collection of Rosse archives from 1540 to 1991 is housed at Birr Castle, with a complete guide and copies available at the Public Record Office Office of Northern Ireland, including family, science and astronomy papers and boxes of family letters, scrapbooks and diaries.

[11] Paul Caffrey, 'Ireland' in Banham, Joanna (ed.) *Enclopeadia of Interior Design*, 2 vols, Fitzroy Dearborn, London and Chicago, 2 Vols, 1997 p. 612 and p. 617.

[12] Information from William Brendan, Earl of Rosse, May 2005.

[13] Oisin Deery, pp. 46, 67.

[14] http://www.entemp.ie/press/1999/221299a.htm.

[15] Oisin Deery, p. 67.

[16] Ibid., pp. 40, 46 and p. 35.

[17] Ibid., p. 47.

[18] Birr Castle Demense, *Fifty Trees of Distinction*, 2nd Ed. 2000 pp. 3–4, 8.

[19] Shirley Nicholson, *Nymans The Story of a Sussex Garden,* Sutton Publishing in association with the National Trust, 2001 ed. p. 90.

[20] Paul Caffrey, p. 619.

[21] Oisin Deery, p. 104.

[22] Ibid., p. 132.

[23] Shirley Nicholson, pp. 92–93.

[24] Notes made by Irene Gilbert for the National Museum of Ireland, after her retirement

[25] Irene Gilbert designed and made the clothes for 'Shake hands with the Devil' in 1959.

[26] Obituary by Pat Crowley, of Irene Gilbert, *Irish Times*, 9 August 1985.

[27] *Irish Times*, 29 August 1985.

[28] Quoted in Robert O'Byrne, 'Couture for a Countess: Lady Rosse's Wardrobe' *Irish Arts Review Yearbook 1996* , vol. 12, pp. 157–63.

[29] As told in interview by the countesses' maid, Margaret Shortt, in the mid-1990s.

[30] As told by Ib Jorgensen, March 2005.

[31] The book to accompany this exhibition is Elizabeth McCrum, *Fashion & form: Irish fashion since 1950,* Sutton Publishing, 1996.

CHAPTER SEVEN

Objects of a passion

The dress worn and collected by Anne, Countess of Rosse, 1935–60

Amy de la Haye

'It ought to be obvious that the objects that occupy our daily lives are in fact the objects of a passion.'[1] Jean Baudrillard

This chapter explores the fashionable dress crafted by London and Paris couturiers that Anne wore, collected and preserved from the date of her marriage to Michael Rosse up to 1960, when her son Antony Armstrong-Jones married Princess Margaret. It also touches upon her continuing passion for fancy dress, and the ceremonial robes she wore in her new role as Countess. Anne had always adored dressing up: now she felt it was her duty to do so.

Anne's dress continues to refer to past fashions and the Messel genealogy, as well as her love of flowers. But some garments tell new stories anticipating future events. Dresses from Anne's trousseau draw stylistically on the indigenous clothing of the couple's honeymoon destinations. Whilst this is often undertaken by visiting royals as a courtesy, it was entirely characteristic of Anne's narrative approach to the dress she wore.

Wedding and honeymoon

Anne and Michael's marriage was blessed at the Church of St Ethelburga the Virgin in London's Bishopsgate, on 19 September 1935. Although

Detail of Jacqmar dress, 1941. *See Plates 72 & 73*

divorce was becoming more acceptable within their social circle, the wedding was a relatively discreet event, with just family and close friends present (Plate 61). Anne wore a pale blue, silk crêpe day dress, which she subsequently packed away in a box along with her bridal accessories (Appendix 246–47): her Duvelleroy purse (Leonard had bought fans from this exclusive Parisian company); fabric flower posy; white heather spray, and ring box (Plate 62). The ceremony might have been understated, but the year-long honeymoon must have made up for it. Their destinations included Paris, Munich, Berlin, Warsaw, Moscow, Colombo, Jakarta, Bali and Peking (Plate 63). Much of Anne's trousseau was made especially for her by Charles James. In the early 1980s Anne told curator Elizabeth Ann Coleman:

> … I still have, amongst my treasured collection (made for my honeymoon in 1935) simple, (yet not really simple!) cotton dresses for the tropics and Far East – stout thick wear for mid-winter in China and Russia – unique designs for desert wear and also dresses for embassy dinners.[2]

All that remains today of these unique creations is the bright yellow bouclé 'Bali' dress – yellow is a colour favoured by young Balinese girls to wear at feasts – featuring a bold red, asymmetric waist detail which references the brightly coloured sashes Balinese women wear on their *kamben* (Plates 64 & 65). A similarly styled dress in Anne's collection is in cream wool with black sash detail (Appendix 169).

Plate 61 Anne and Michael Rosse's wedding, 1935. (From Anne's scrapbook)

Plate 62 Wedding ephemera, 1935.

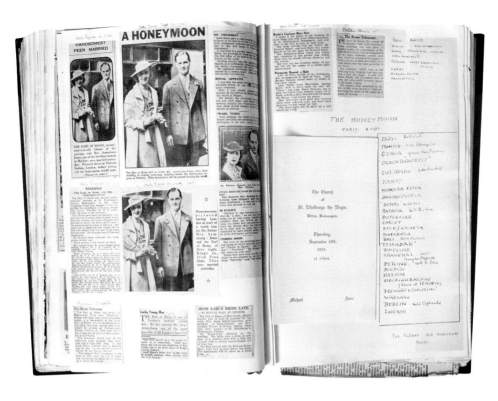

Plate 63 Anne and Michael Rosse's honeymoon, 1935. (From Anne's scrapbook)

From the innovative Paris couturière Elsa Schiaparelli's 'Stop, Look, Listen' collection, shown in February 1935, Anne ordered a 'sari' evening dress, cut and draped to spiral around the feminine body. This design was available in a vibrant palette, combining vivid blue with 'desert pink', and some models featured beaded borders.[3] Anne's dress is in cream silk with bright blue panels and tails, devoid of embellishment. As Schiaparelli had opened her London salon in Upper Grosvenor Street, in 1934, it is possible that Anne ordered the dress there, along with a white silk crêpe evening dress, both frequently worn and now very fragile (Appendix 196–97). The latter dress was packed away with the written recollection: 'Darling Michael loved me in this dress. I wore it mostly on my honeymoon, Schiaparelli 1935.'

In China, Anne and Michael visited Michael's mother, and Robert Byron, a contemporary of Michael's at Oxford who went on to write travel diaries from Persia and Afghanistan, and with whom they helped establish The Georgian Group in 1937. In Peking the couple stayed with Harold Acton and visited Michael's younger brother, the Hon. Desmond Parsons, an internationally respected Chinese scholar and collector who was teaching at Peking University. Desmond was incurably ill, and Michael and Anne accompanied him home to Birr, along with his precious collection of Chinese artifacts, on the Trans-Siberian railway. Desmond died in 1937; his three enormous cedar wood trunks, two of which still contain scrolls of paintings and a group of Chinese garments (Appendix 232), have been preserved in the family collection.[4]

Fig. 41 Oliver Messel The Earl and Countess of Rosse at Birr Castle, undated.
Private Collection. Photograph: Photographic Survey, Courtauld Institute of Art

Anne and Michael's marriage was by all accounts a supremely happy union (Fig. 41) and the couple had two sons, William Brendan (born Lord Oxmantown, 1936) and Martin (the Hon. Martin Parsons, born 1938). Anne and Michael's close friend John Cornforth – the architecture editor for *Country Life*, observed:

> Michael had a noble, Whig, sense of idealism that was part of his
> Parsons inheritance. Anne's approach was complementary, and in
> a way more down to earth, because she appreciated her father's
> attitude to work and was proud of the Jewish elements in her
> background and own personality.[5]

Although Birr was their main residence, the couple also spent time in London and North Yorkshire, the location of Womersley Hall, which had passed by descent into the Rosse family in the mid-nineteenth century. Uninhabited since 1921, the house had fallen into disrepair and many of the original furnishings had been sold – even the drawing-room floor had been ripped up and auctioned.[6] Womersley Hall, which was to become another of Anne's refurbishment projects, was her wartime refuge and a place she became deeply attached to. It was the site where she and Michael chose eventually to be laid to rest together, and the Dowager Viscountess de Vesci (Michael's mother, who had re-married into this distinguished Irish family in 1920) lived there until she died in 1984.

above Plate 64 Detail of 'Bali dress' by
Charles James, 1935.

right Plate 65 Anne, Countess of Rosse's 'Bali
dress' by Charles James, 1935.

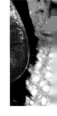

Dressing the part: jewels and Coronation robes

When Anne became the Countess of Rosse she inherited the magnificent Rosse jewels – a diamond and emerald tiara, necklace and earrings which Charles Castle describes as 'possibly the finest in the world'.[7] Photographic portraits reveal that Anne wore these with great panache. Dorothy Wilding's portrait was reproduced for the covers of *The Tatler*[8] and *The Queen*[9] in 1939 (Fig. 42), both of which Anne mounted in her album. Wilding was a leading society portrait photographer.

Anne's album also contains a portrait from the *Sketch* which showed her looking resplendent in robes and coronet for the Coronation of King George VI. The editorial noted that '… her robes, over 100 years old, were worn with the Rosse tiara and necklaces of emeralds and diamonds which had been in her husband's family since the reign of Queen Anne [1702–14]'.[10] Anne wore a close-fitting open robe (kirtle) of crimson velvet trimmed with miniver fur at the front edge, with short sleeves and a small cape across the shoulders, which of course followed the correct sumptuary rules for this ceremonial dress. The length of the train, and the width of the ermine trim, along with the design of the coronet, varied with social status. As a Countess, Anne's robe had a one-and-a-half-yard train and three inches of fur edging. Peeresses' coronets are of the same design but smaller than those worn by peers; Anne wore a silver circlet with eight strawberry leaves alternating with eight silver balls raised on points (Fig. 44).[11]

It would seem that Anne's approach towards the jewellery she wore echoed her fashion preoccupations. John Cornforth observed: 'Perhaps from her father she inherited her love of old jewellery and she appreciated it for its design and its history and associations.'[12] Anne also owned a large, Art Nouveau-style dragonfly brooch (which she wore from the 1940s to the '60s) and a constellation of five star-shaped diamond brooches. Clearly aware of the interest her behaviour generated, on some occasions she wore the brooches on the back of her coat, commenting that it would be nice for other people to see them whilst she was talking to someone else; at other times she wore them circling her neckline.[13] An alluring portrait taken by the Bassano studio in May 1936 shows Anne wearing a fringed bib gold necklace, a style that was highly fashionable, with an asymmetric draped blouse (Fig. 43). Cornforth recalled that, much later in Anne's life, 'Even sitting up in a hospital bed she would be wearing more pearls round her neck and wrists than most people would wear to a dance, and she was one of those rare people who planned their clothes around their jewels.'[14]

Margaret Shortt, who came to work at Birr in 1945 and was to become Anne's lady's maid, told Robert O'Byrne that it took Anne about two hours to dress for the day. 'She was very, very particular … everything had to be right … she really loved dressing up for evenings and special occasions.'[15] There were, of course, many of these.

Fig. 42 Dorothy Wilding portrait of Anne, Countess of Rosse wearing the Rosse emeralds, 1935.

Fig. 43 Bassano studio portrait of Anne, Countess of Rosse, 1935. *National Portrait Gallery, London*

Fig. 44 Anne, Countess of Rosse in her Coronation robes, 1937.

London couture

Anne continued to champion the talents of London couturiers. A recent discovery within the family collection is a box containing a mauve-pink silk evening dress with finely stitched tucked bands and a matching capelet (the latter very fashionable in the early 1930s) by Peter Russell, who had opened a salon at 1 Bruton Street (formerly occupied by Charles James) in 1931. Anne's hand-written memo dates the dress to 1933; today it has virtually perished (Appendix 195).

The most understated surviving evening dress worn by Anne during this period is made in black silk chiffon with long cuffed sleeves, designed in 1937 by the Anglo-Irish couturier Edward Molyneux. Molyneux (like Norman Hartnell) worked with Lucile, prior to opening salons in London (48 Grosvenor Street) and Paris in 1919. Molyneux's interests would have undoubtedly appealed to Anne: as well as designing couture fashion, he was a gifted artist whose own paintings were inspired by his private collection of Impressionist landscape and flower paintings.[16] Anne's dress is a superb example of Molyneux's deceptively simple designs, often executed in dark or neutral tones. Interest is achieved from clever cutting and drapery rather than extraneous detailing or decoration. With its shapely silhouette, swathed around the hip and hinting at late nineteenth and early twentieth-century fashions, Anne's choice of understated 'little black dress' was entirely characteristic (Appendix 202).

Charles James's evening gowns, 1935–39: 'challenging and exquisite'

In spite of her flawless figure, which would have displayed to great advantage the fashionable bias-cut gowns which skimmed and encircled the feminine body, Anne continued to favour for special occasions structured neo-Victorian styles, usually designed by Charles James. His evening gowns, which Anne considered both 'challenging and exquisite',[17] featured corsetry, crinoline and bustle-style skirts, unusual colour mixes and seductive drapery (which often served to conceal the gown's rigid inner structure). Anne's dresses were often made in *ingénue* glistening silk satins in a pale, shell-like palette, in contrast to the stronger colours and bolder patterns she came to favour in the 1950s.

An evening gown from 1936 is executed in a sophisticated combination of ice blue, pale rose and amber silk satin, with shoestring shoulder straps, central cornucopia folds, laced back and flared skirt, and a matching stole (Plate 66). This dress is not only a superb example of James's refined fashion aesthetic and flawless couture craftsmanship, it might also have special significance for the Messel Dress Collection. During the process of examining the collection in its entirety for the first time, the possibility has been raised that its unusual colouration might

have links to a dress of about 1874 worn by Marion Sambourne (see Conclusion).[8]

In 1937, Anne wore a Charles James corselette dress (also known as *la Sylphide*) which was inspired by an 1850s silhouette and updated with an external, back-lacing, hour-glass 'corset' and a floral corsage. This model was featured in American *Vogue* in June 1937, in lilac organza, and was also available in canary yellow.[19] Anne eschewed colour and commissioned her dress in cream-coloured silk (Appendix 201). She later used the detachable 'corset' as a pattern for a calico corset, which she probably made herself. On the inside is pencilled 'Merle Oberon – used Shakespeare play' (Appendix 254). Oberon had starred with Douglas Fairbanks Snr. in the film *The Private Life of Don Juan* (1934), and co-starred with Leslie Howard in *The Scarlet Pimpernel* (1935), both of which had been produced by London Films with costumes designed by Oliver Messel.[20] This annotated garment reveals a clear link between Oliver, Merle Oberon and Anne, Countess of Rosse, but its nature has not been established.

A black silk faille evening dress from 1937 – known by the family as *Coq Noir* – is distinguished from Anne's otherwise prettily romantic Charles James evening dresses, although it retains her penchant for bustles. It is full length, with an asymmetrical front neckline, crossover-strap, back V-neckline and a crescent-shaped bustle which is set to one side and supported with nylon *crin* (a meshed interlining) (Appendix 200). This is a complex garment to put on and wear, but both designer and client prioritised beauty and impact over ease and comfort. As Anne stated:

> To begin with, there could be a mystery as to how to get into the clothes when they arrived! Or which was the front or the back, which he might have altered at the last moment! With some, walking might be difficult – or sitting tricky! But an appreciative wearer would gladly cooperate.[21]

This dress has been worn in more recent years by Lady Alicia Parsons, Anne's granddaughter.

Anne's albums of press cuttings and personal ephemera reveal that in 1938 she and Michael Rosse travelled to South Carolina, Mexico and New York: she kept several of the Charles James dresses she wore that year. In New York, the couple were guests of honour at a dinner party hosted by Cecil Beaton at his apartment in the Waldorf Astoria. Whilst there, Anne wore a romantic ball gown in cream silk satin trimmed with black velvet ribbon and black Chantilly lace, with a garland design (the materials are suggestive of lingerie) (Plate 67). With its sweetheart neckline, wide décolletage, fitted bodice and polonaise effect, it is evocative of early 1870s fashions. Anne was photographed by Horst wearing this dress for an article entitled 'Individualists' which appeared in

right Plate 66 Dress by Charles James, 1936. Worn by Anne Rosse at the Holland House Ball.

Plate 67 Dress by Charles James, 1938.

American *Vogue* (Fig. 45). 'Decidedly Victorian are the evening dresses worn by the Countess of Rosse ...' reads the editorial. 'This white satin one, all lace flounces, velvet bows, and padded bustle, was made – as are all her clothes – by Charles James'.[22]

A Charles James design that is probably unique is Anne's 'Snow White' silk twill day dress, from 1938, the year after Walt Disney's critically acclaimed 'Snow White and the Seven Dwarfs' was premiered in the United States (Plate 68). Popular Hollywood films spawned lucrative themed merchandise, and Anne's printed silk is a refined example of this output. Novelty prints featuring unusual motifs on dark grounds were highly fashionable in 1937–38. There is a family photograph which shows Anne wearing the dress (Fig. 46), which was subsequently worn by her daughter Susan. Unlike the dresses that Anne acquired from James's seasonal collections, the clothes he made specifically for her show signs of being hastily put together. Not surprisingly they are unlabelled, but they clearly convey the couturier's inimitable stylistic signatures and their provenance is given further credence from Anne's archives and the hand-written labelling and

Fig. 45 Horst portrait of Anne, Countess of Rosse wearing Charles James, in US *Vogue*, 15 May, 1938. *Horst / Vogue / © The Condé Nast Publications Inc.*

Plate 68 Anne, Countess of Rosse's 'Snow White' dress
by Charles James, 1938.

Fig. 46 Anne, Countess of Rosse with Susan and Antony
Armstrong-Jones and William Brendan, Lord Oxmantown,
1938.

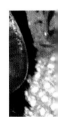

Plate 69 Detail of 'Snow White' dress by Charles
James, 1938.

descriptions on the boxes that house them.

Anne also adored Charles James's dramatic evening coats and cloaks. She lent to the Brooklyn Museum exhibition her (labelled) 1938, full-length, black velvet evening coat with black tassels and decorative swirls of black stitching (Appendix 240), which is still housed in the collection. Anne loved capes with a medieval fantasy feel. A Charles James 'spider' cape was recently brought to light from the family collection, probably made from an early form of nylon and dating from 1937 (Appendix 239).[23] Another cape, fully circular – not by Charles James – is made in deep blue velvet with a pearl encrusted, gilded collar and gold tassel decoration at the back, which dates from the mid-to-late 1930s (Plate 70). It is rather ecclesiastical in appearance and could serve as both dramatic fashionable dress (Molyneux, Marcel Rochas and Schiaparelli were also designing capes with tassels and similarly ornate decoration in 1935) or fancy dress. There are three other unattributed velvet capes in the family collection from this period: one in black with a gold collar, another in violet, and the third in deep purple velvet with a silver embroidered shawl collar, and a matching bag embroidered 'Anne' bearing a decorative crown above her name. Anne may well have worked this embroidery herself. There is also a short, tiered, orange wool cape, said to be made by Anne, and which she wore to have her portrait painted by Cecil Beaton, both of which are in the family collection (Appendix 234–38).

In 1939, Anne wore James's 'ribbon dress' to the Duchess of Marlborough's Blenheim Ball. Made in palest pink silk faille and flesh-toned organza, it has crossover shoestring shoulder straps and a *bouillone* skirt (over stiff tulle underskirts) in clear 1870s style, looped with a multiplicity of bright, multi-coloured, bow-tied ribbons (Plate 57). By this time, Charles James was internationally heralded as an extraordinarily talented and innovative couturier, but he remained infuriatingly unreliable in terms of completing his orders and his business administration in general. In 1974 Diana Vreeland, a former editor of *Vogue*, commented wryly that 'He would far rather work and rework a beautiful dress ordered for a certain party than have that dress appear at the party.'[24]

Anne recalled:

Understandably there came a day when the bailiffs came into Bruton Street and his beautiful collection was quickly thrown into taxis at six or seven in the morning, for me to find piled up on the floors of my little dining room as I was preparing a luncheon party! Such was his generosity that he wanted to give me the lot in the end.[25]

In 1939 Charles James once again relocated to New York. There is no evidence that Anne wore his designs after this date.

above Plate 70 Evening cloak, back view, mid-to-late 1930s.

right Plate 71 'Ribbon dress' by Charles James, 1939.

Fancy dress

Anne continued to attend costumes balls dressed in styles based around the 1770–1820 period. In September 1951 she and Oliver, possibly accompanied by Michael, attended the famous eighteenth-century costume ball given by the millionaire Charles de Bestegui to celebrate his newly restored Palazzo Labia, which had outstanding frescoes by Tiepolo. The occasion marked the launch of the first Venice Film Festival. Castle sets the scene:

> Lady Diana Cooper, acting as hostess for Bestegui, received his
> guests in a Cleopatra costume of delicate silver-blue with panniers
> of old rose, designed by Oliver [Messel] in the style of Tiepolo,
> and a wig designed by Stanley Hall. The Aga Khan, wearing the
> robes of an Eastern potentate, was the escort of Princess Radziwill
> … and Oliver attended in a rich red velvet uniform coat which
> had once belonged to a Bohemian Prince.[26]

Lord Rosse remarks that his mother often spoke about this party, hailed by *Vogue* as a 'landmark in entertaining',[27] recollecting that some guests arrived on elephants, whilst Salvador Dalí made a sensational entrance to the ball in a costume designed by Dior.[28] Unfortunately, we do not know which dress Anne wore.

In August 1939 Anne attended the famous Georgian Ball at Osterley House, Lord and Lady Jersey's home with its series of Robert Adam interiors. Clearly distinctive even by Anne's standards, in his biography of Robert Byron, James Fox noted that 'Anne Rosse, who never did things by halves, coloured not only her hair but also her eyelids and eyelashes blue'.[29] The ball was reviewed in *Vogue* (Fig. 47) with an accompanying article enititled 'Neo Georgian Ball Gowns'[30] in which Anne was photographed by Rawlings wearing a black velvet and cream silk satin gown by Hartnell, with faux pearls and diamond studded lace, complete with 1770s-style wig.

By the late 1930s, Hartnell had sealed his reputation as a designer of historically inspired fashions. In 1938 he was invited to design the clothes for the Queen's state visit to Paris. At the King's request, he based his designs on the 1850s and '60s crinoline gowns depicted in royal portraits by the artist Franz Xaver Winterhalter (1805–73) which, at the time, hung in Buckingham Palace. Hartnell recalled: 'His Majesty made it clear in his quiet way that I should attempt to capture this picturesque grace in the dresses I was to design for the Queen.'[31]

In October of 1938, *Vogue* declared:

> Make no mistake, you'll be wearing, as a matter of course, clothes
> that a year ago would have seemed pure fancy dress, notably
> crinolines, authentic hoops, strapless bodices, bustle backs … You

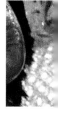

Fig. 47 Anne, Countess of Rosse at the Georgian Ball Osterley Park, seated second row from back wearing a 'Gainsborough hat', in *Vogue*, 9 August, 1939. *Vogue* / © *The Condé Nast Publications Inc.*

may have one *à la Eugénie* or a Victorian – but have one you must: they are truly contemporary.[32]

This was, of course, a style that Anne had already perfected.

On 3 September of that year Britain and France declared war on Germany.

Second World War

Throughout the Second World War the Messel family, like many others, was separated for many years. Nicholson records that Leonard and Maud's eldest son, Linley, served in the Middle East, becoming a Lieutenant-Colonel, whilst his brother Oliver was a captain in the Camouflage Unit of the Royal Engineers.[33] Michael Rosse, in the footsteps of his father (who was killed in the First World War when Michael was twelve), joined the Irish Guards. As a Captain he served as an Intelligence Officer in the Guards' Armoured Division, whose official story he co-authored. He fought from the Normandy landings of June 1944 through to the battle of Nijmegen in September 1944.[34]

James Lees-Milne remembered seeing Anne:

> … during the war in a hospital ward, her head tied in a charwoman's turban, vigorously scrubbing the floor on hands and knees while enchanting the other ladies engaged in the same occupation with her jokes and fun.[35]

Thus Anne – as did her mother Maud, despite her advancing years – actively undertook work to support the war effort wherever she lived: at Nymans, at Womersley or at Birr. Anne took her family to the safety of Womersley and set about making it not only habitable but stylish and comfortable. The Birr scrapbooks show that she undertook war duties in nearby Pontefract, visiting hospitals and undertaking Red Cross work, whilst evacuees were given homes both at Womersley and at Nymans. With gardens always on her mind, Anne inveigled the soldiers billeted in the grounds to dig over the Womersley garden.[36]

Nicholson records, however, that the gardens at Nymans had to be run down during the war, with the younger gardeners being called up for military service and no heating available for the hothouses.[37] Anne's passport confirms her travels across the Irish Sea throughout this period. A press cutting dated 27 November, 1943, from an unidentified Irish newspaper in the Birr Archives, states that, 'In addition to her work for WUS and the Red Cross in England, the Countess of Rosse has, since the beginning of the war, organised and run a hospital and supply for the Irish Red Cross at Birr Castle.'

However, as well as stress and duty, there was also fun to be had, as is revealed in a classic Anne-style note to be pinned onto a wartime evening dress. 'Had a wonderful time in this dress am ashamed to say. 1941!!' (Plate 72). This is one of the few surviving garments from these years. It is made in dark green crêped wool with short sleeves, and is trimmed with a stylish decorative neckline of berry-like clusters of purple painted glass droplets, with green glass leaves and burgundy-coloured looped chenille thread (Plate 73). The dress carries a Jacqmar label. Although Anne wore it in 1941, she may have purchased it beforehand as

left Plate 72 Wool dress by Jacqmar belonging to Anne, Countess of Rosse, 1941.

above Plate 73 Detail of Jacqmar dress, 1941.

it flouts wartime Utility regulations, though designers and clients did circumvent these rulings by using up pre-existing materials. The styling of the dress, with its broad, padded shoulders, is in keeping both with designs from 1938 and wartime trends. Jacqmar was fashionably based at 16 Grosvenor Street, in London, and became internationally famous after the war for its silk and wool fashion fabrics and printed scarves. From 1939 Bianca Mosca, a member of the Utility fashion design team during the war who had formerly worked with Schiaparelli in Paris, directed the Jacqmar studio and may have designed this dress. However, Anne was more than capable of adding the beaded decoration herself.

As the war came to an end, family life slowly re-established itself. Old commitments were picked up and new ones developed; in 1943 Michael Rosse had became Chairman of the National Trust's Historic Building Committee.[38] A group of Anne's silk day dresses survive from the late 1940s, all in shades of blue (Appendix 172–73). There are two pretty and colourful print dresses, still with broad shoulders, and a longer skirt and blouse possibly from about 1948–50 in bright blue, with colourful red and pink roses printed on the hemline and appliquéd on the blouse – possibly by Anne.

After the war, Anne travelled abroad quite extensively: her passport shows that she went to Switzerland and Paris in 1948, and to Berlin in 1950.

A family tradition: Anne makes dresses for Susan

Plate 74 Detail of Susan, Viscountess de Vesci's dress, 1953.

On 20 May, 1950, Susan, Anne's daughter from her first marriage, married John Eustace Vesey, 6th Viscount de Vesci of Abbey Leix County Laois, Ireland. With consummate style and skill Anne made, and subsequently preserved, Susan's wedding dress (Appendix 280). On the inside waistband Anne partially hand-embroidered and pencilled 'to my darling Susan'. Susan and her husband were to have four children, Emma Frances (1951), Catherine Anne (1953), Thomas Eustace (1955) and Georgina Mary (1963). Sadly Georgina died two years after her birth.

Anne made and preserved another dress that she made for Susan, to wear to the Queen's first party, in 1953. It is in bright yellow silk twill and features a prominent, bright pink-red silk camellia – a family flower – at the bottom centre neckline (a striking combination which brings to mind Anne's 'Bali' dress). (Plate 60) Anne attached a hastily hand-written luggage label to the box that housed it, which reads 'Susan Dress. I sat up and made in Bridget's flat in Mount Street for a sudden invitation to Buck Pal...'

These, along with the linen Sybil Connolly dress (Appendix 278) are the only surviving garments belonging to Susan.

1953: Coronation and the Coronation Ball
(Anne wears a silk designed by Oliver)

For the Coronation of Queen Elizabeth II in June 1953, Norman Hartnell was invited to design new robes for the peeresses, comprising a kirtle of crimson velvet, cut with a small train and no sleeves, but with a deep shawl collar in miniver or coney. Given her appreciation of clothing with history and 'meaning' it is not surprising that Anne chose to wear the traditional robe she had worn for the previous Coronation. Oliver made a small maquette of Anne to mark the occasion (Plate 75) and painted her wearing her robes.

Anne chose John Cavanagh – the youngest and arguably the most innovative of London's 'top eleven' couturiers – to design the dress she would wear to the Coronation Ball. Cavanagh had trained with Molyneux (in London and Paris) during the 1930s and, after serving in the war, joined Pierre Balmain in 1947. He returned to London in 1952 and opened his own couture salon at 26 Curzon Street.

Anne's dress was made in a commemorative silk originally designed by Oliver for the Hungarian émigré Nicholas 'Miki' Sekers, who had founded West Cumberland Silks in 1938. Sekers was exceptional among United Kingdom textiles manufacturers for his astute fashion sense. By the 1950s, his clientele included Dior and Balenciaga. Sekers had seen Oliver's stage sets for the Glyndebourne Festival Opera in 1952, where he (Sekers) was a Founding Trustee.

Sekers recorded that Oliver was initially unwilling to take on this commission due to his lack of knowledge of textiles technicalities. 'We explained that this was precisely the reason that we were asking him – we wanted something absolutely new from someone of his artistic calibre and genius.'[39]

Oliver relented and six of his designs were put into production: 'Jewels', 'Scattered Leaves', 'Acorn', 'Miniver', 'Juliette' and 'Twigs', in colours described at the time as nugget gold, white gold, mother-of-pearl, grey, navy blue, lime, candy pink and a rich vermillion. To weave the designs, Sekers introduced a new technique by which two gossamer silks were joined together by embroidered designs, some using real gold and silver thread. Oliver's textile designs were also utilised by London couturiers Hartnell, Hardy Amies, Worth and Ronald Paterson.

Cavanagh's 1953 Coronation collection showcased 'Acorn' and 'Jewel'. The couturier used these patterned silks towards the back of his gowns, featuring magnolia silk satin on the necklines and bodices to provide a plain ground for the priceless heirloom jewels his clients would be wearing. Anne's dress, entirely made from Oliver's fabric, has a round neckline with a gathered heart-shaped 'bustier' effect underneath. The dress is lightly boned, with a high waist, zip fastening, a flared skirt draped over the hip and a train (Plate 76).

Plate 75 Oliver Messel maquette of Anne, Countess of Rosse in Coronation robes, 1953.

right Plate 76 Dress by John Cavanagh belonging to Anne, Countess of Rosse, 1953.

Family homes

Anne continued to make occasional use of the London house at 18 Stafford Terrace after the war. Reena Suleman comments that it became 'her London *pied à terre*', and she carefully;

> … integrated the required improvements in a largely sympathetic manner, repairing and restoring the historic fabric of the home wherever possible. This pragmatic approach pre-dated the modern conservation movement and Anne's foresight led to the founding of the Victorian Society at 18 Stafford Terrace in 1957.[40]

We know from both diaries and the memoirs of her friends that they attended meetings, dinners and soirées at the house throughout this period. John Cornforth recalled Anne's skill as a hostess:

> Those dark crowded rooms would glow with a wonderful warmth and people would feel happy in them. But often it was the details of the evening that remained most vivid for me – a late supper with an épergne on the table beneath the skirted lamp in the dining room and, although it was winter, the épergne was filled with violets and round it were clusters of violets in little pots. That was typical of Anne's creative imagination, her sense of detail and the trouble she would take over everything, even if it was just for one evening. Similarly I remember a pouringly wet summer's day at Nymans when the table was carpeted with camellias and laid with old Chinese blue and white china, and, not content with that, on the table were the cups won for the camellias, each one encircled with the correct flowers.[41]

Anne continued to work on restoring Womersley. In 1958 she invited the interior decorator John Fowler to paint the drawing room. Fowler was raising traditionalist eyebrows at the time with his penchant for brilliant colour schemes within eighteenth-century buildings. However, whilst for each of them it went against the grain of their love of dramatic and theatrical interiors, subtle tones were chosen to harmonise with the rest of the interiors and to retain the character of the building.[42]

1960: Antony marries Princess Margaret

After attending Eton and reading architecture at Cambridge, Anne's son Antony Armstrong-Jones established himself as a highly successful photographer. Encouraged by Oliver, he had started his career taking photographs of people in the theatre, and went on to become acclaimed

Plate 77 Ensemble worn by Anne, Countess of Rosse at the marriage of Antony Armstrong-Jones to Princess Margaret, 1960.

Plate 78 Wedding photograph of
Princess Margaret to Antony
Armstrong-Jones ,1960.
Photograph by Cecil Beaton,
© Camera Press Ltd London

for his irreverent fashion photographs, informal society portraits and
sensitive documentary photographs, as well as a working as a designer
and an Emmy award-winning documentary film-maker. Through his work,
which encompassed the world of art, theatre and High Society, he met
the Queen's sister, Princess Margaret, whom he married in 1960.

The ceremony took place at Westminster Abbey on 6 May, 1960.
Princess Margaret wore a white organza dress with fitted bodice and very
full skirt, designed by Hartnell: her sole ornament was the magnificent
Poltimore diamond tiara. Antony wore a morning suit, the customary
dress for a non-royal groom.

For the wedding Anne wore a suit designed by London couturier
Victor Stiebel, who also designed Princess Margaret's primrose-yellow
going-away outfit. Stiebel had studied architecture at Cambridge where,
like Norman Hartnell, he had developed a passion for dress design whilst
creating costumes for the 'Footlights Revue'. After training at Reville
between 1929 and 1932, Stiebel opened his own London house at 21
Bruton Street. From the outset, Stiebel aligned himself with the 1930s
vogue for period styles that Anne so loved: in 1933 she had been
photographed at his 'Midnight Intimate Party' wearing a gown with what
Harper's Bazaar described as a 'Victorian décolletage'.[43] During the war,
Stiebel's business had been run by the Jacqmar organisation while Stiebel
himself was in the forces. When he was de-mobilised he joined Jacqmar
as director of couture. In 1958 he re-launched his own couture house in
a magnificent eighteenth-century building at 17 Cavendish Square.

Anne chose to wear a matching Stiebel dress and coat ensemble in
oyster-coloured silk brocade,an unconventional 'colour' for the mother of
the groom (Plate 77). The coat has a black fur shawl collar and she
lamented in a hand-written note: 'The coat had a beautiful black mink
collar which I could not afford to buy.' The London College of Fashion

houses Stiebel's album of 1960s designs, and inspection shows that this ensemble is entirely distinctive, created exclusively for Anne to wear on this prestigious occasion (Appendix 249).

She accessorised the ensemble with a monochrome hat in nylon filament thread, designed by Simone Mirman, who had worked with Schiaparelli in Paris prior to opening her own millinery establishment in London in 1947 (Appendix 250). The outfit was obviously a great success – Anne wrote a note on Birr Castle headed paper: 'This was acclaimed by the world as the smartest.'

Anne and her former husband Ronald sat together during the service and then followed down the aisle behind the Royal Party to drive in procession through cheering crowds to Buckingham Palace. The official photograph was taken by Cecil Beaton (Plate 78) and a review appeared in *Vogue* of June 1960,[44] with drawings by the Polish artist Felix Topolski. At Nymans the staff were given the day off, with free beer to toast the couple's good health: along with millions of other people around the globe, they watched the event broadcast on television.[45] When, eighteen months later, Antony was created Earl of Snowdon, he was also granted the subsidiary title of Viscount Linley of Nymans.

Conclusion

Anne preserved about fifty of the outfits she wore between 1935 and 1960. In the five years before the Second World War it was mostly her Charles James dresses that she kept. As she told the John Morley, Director of the Royal Pavilion, '… the fact that I've treasured these things is proof of what I thought of them.'[46] In the postwar period, it was primarily the garments by Irish designers, notably Irene Gilbert, that she retained. She also carefully packed away dress and related ephemera that she associated with rites of passage and those clothes she made for herself and her daughter. Whether purchased from a couturier, made or embellished by her own hand, Anne's clothes were always intensely personal. Her son the Earl of Snowdon noted,

> … unlike nowadays when people just go off and buy clothes from a particular designer, she was *totally* involved in anything made for her. She could – and did – add a lot.[47]

I am grateful to Lou Taylor for research on the Second World War section and Eleanor Thompson on fancy dress clothes

[1] Jean Baudrillard, 'The System of Collecting' in Elsner, John and Cardinal, Roger, *The Cultures of Collecting*, Melbourne University Press, Australia, 1994, p. 7.

[2] Elizabeth Coleman Anne, *The Genius of Charles James*, The Brooklyn Museum, New York, 1982, p. 111.

[3] Dilys Blum, *Schiaparelli*, Philadelphia Museum of Art, USA, 2004, p. 72.

[4] See Conclusion.

[5] John Cornforth, 'An Address Given By John Cornforth at the Church of St. Martin Womersley, Doncaster, Yorkshire, on 9 July 1992', at the funeral of Anne, Countess of Rosse, Nymans Archives.

[6] Unattributed articles by Marcus Binney and Olive Coombe, Nymans.

[7] Charles Castle, *Oliver Messel: A Biography*, Thames & Hudson, London, 1986, p. 145.

[8] *The Tatler*, 2 August 1939.

[9] *The Queen*, 6 December 1939.

[10] *Sketch*, 1937, p. 405 (Anne's album).

[11] Una Campbell, with a forword by H.R.H. The Prince of Wales, *Robes of the Realm: 300 Years of Ceremonial Dress*, Michael O'Mara Books Ltd, London, 1989, pp. 49–50.

[12] John Cornforth, *op. cit.*, 1992.

[13] Robert O'Byrne, 'Couture for a Countess: Lady Rosse's Wardrobe', *Irish Arts Review Yearbook* 1996, volume 12, pp. 161–63.

[14] John Cornforth, *op. cit.*, 1992.

[15] Robert O'Byrne, p. 158.

[16] Mary Picken, *Dressmakers of France*, Harper Brothers, New York, 1956, pp. 53–54.

[17] Elizabeth Anne Coleman, *op. cit.*, 1982, p. 111.

[18] This hypothesis is discussed further in the Conclusion.

[19] There is an example of this in the V&A Furniture, Textiles & Dress Collection.

[20] Pinkham, Roger, *Oliver Messel*, V&A, London, 1983: 185.

[21] Elizabeth Anne Coleman, *op. cit.*, 1982, p. 111.

[22] American *Vogue*, 15 May 1938, p. 62.

[23] See Conclusion.

[24] 'Portrait of a Genius by a Genius, Charles James and his Friends', *Nova*, July 1974, p. 51.

[25] Elizabeth Anne Coleman, *op. cit.*, 1982, p. 112.

[26] Charles Castle, *op. cit.*, 1986, p. 155.

[27] *Vogue*, November 1951, p. 97.

[28] Lord Rosse, Interview, June 2004.

[29] James Fox, *Robert Byron,* Murray, London, 2003, p. 357.

[30] *Vogue,* 23 August 1939, pp. 28–29.

[31] Norman Hartnell, *Silver & Gold*, Evans, London, 1955, p. 94.

[32] *Vogue*, October 1938.

[33] Shirley Nicholson, *Nymans: the story of a Sussex garden*, Sutton Publishing/National Trust, Gloucestershire, p. 102.

[34] Earl of Rosse and E.R. Hill, *The story of the Guards Armoured Division, 1941–1945*, Geoffrey Bles, London, 1956.

[35] James Lees-Milne, Obituary for Anne Rosse, The *Independent*, 8 July 1992

[36] Article on sale of Womersley by Marcus Binney, Nymans Archive.

[37] Shirley Nicholson, *op. cit.*, p. 100.

[38] *Oliver Messel and Other Designs in Sekers Fabrics*, exhibition leaflet, Incorporated Society of London Fashion Designers, 1953.

[39] Shirley Nicholson, *op. cit.*, p. 100.

[40] Reena Suleman from text provided.

[41] John Cornforth, *op. cit.*, 1992.

[42] Article on sale of Womersley, ibid.

[43] See Chapter 5.

[44] *Vogue*, June 1960, pp. 57–61.

[45] Shirley Nicholson, *op. cit.*, p. 12.

[46] Letter from Anne, Countess of Rosse to John Morley c.June 1981. Museum reference: coll/9/d/i.

[47] The Earl of Snowdon, quoted in O'Byrne, Robert, 'Couture for a Countess: Lady Rosse's Wardrobe', *Irish Arts Review*, Yearbook 1996, vol. 12, p. 157.

CONCLUSION

The Fifth and Sixth Generations

Heritage, memory, dispersal and the survival of the Messel Dress Collection

Lou Taylor

Our exploration of the material culture of the clothes of six generations of women from the Sambourne/Messel/Rosse family drew to a close in the spring of 2005. At that point the last group of family garments came to the light of day, from the family estate of Womersley in Yorkshire,[1] the home of the Hon. Martin Parsons. While it was up for sale in 2004, a final, fascinating group of garments was found. These included a dark red, fur-trimmed, velvet house coat worn by Michael Rosse, labelled 'Balmain, Paris'; the bold green, pink and white floral art-deco shawl, discussed in Chapter 5 and the famous little black veiled cocktail hat by one of London's most famous 1930s–50s milliners, Aage Thaarup, in which Anne was sketched by Charles Baskerville (Fig. 48) (Appendix 277 & 261).

More Charles James items emerged, including a black and white version of the yellow and red 'Bali' dress of 1935 and the transparent, shiny black evening cloak, 'Spider wrap', by Charles James (Appendix 239). There were also two curiously cut, silk check print blouses, formed like Möbius strips and very probably an experiment by Charles James (or Anne herself), dating from the later 1930s (Appendix 190–91). A vivid, royal-blue silk skirt and bodice, dating probably from the late 1940s, features bright red and pink printed and appliquéd roses (Appendix 172). A turquoise-toned, silk floral print dress from the late 1940s emerged too, which matches one at Birr as well as two smart, simple, collarless linen summer suits in soft blue and cream-coloured linen (Appendix 173, 180–81).

Detail of Chinese ceremonial vest. *See Plate 64*

Finally out of the tissue paper came two treasures, which epitomise the unique and sophisticated quality of this entire eclectic collection. The first was yet another glamorous, full-length evening dress designed by Irene Gilbert, of about 1960 (Plate 79). This one is made in white silk, with wide shoulder straps. The fabric is covered entirely with large, shocking-pink carnations with black stems and leaves, hand embroidered in heavy cotton. One flower is carefully cut out and appliquéd on the centre from of the bodice, much like Maud's application of a Nymans embroidery to the front of her 1906–08 *Mascotte* dress (Plates 37 & 38).

The second treasure is a spectacular deeply fringed Chinese vest, for a woman, possibly from the eighteenth century. In dark blue silk, it is sleeveless, woven and embroidered with sacred symbols. Applied on the back is the insignia badge for the wife of a fifth-rank civil official – a silver pheasant, shown with cloud formations, and rolling wave forms in satin stitch and couching.[2] Typically of the Countess of Rosse, the front panel has been removed but was carefully wrapped and kept close by (Plates 80 & 81). This garment could possibly have been worn by Anne and is almost certainly from the large collection of Chinese textiles put together in Beijing in the early 1930s by the Hon. Desmond Parsons, as discussed in Chapter 7. Other Chinese garments and textiles survive at Birr Castle.

Fig. 48 Charles Baskerville portrait of Anne, Countess of Rosse wearing Aage Thaarup hat, mid-1930s. *Private Collection. Photograph: Photographic Survey, Courtauld Institute of Art*

Family heritage

These last 'finds' confirmed our previous 'reading' of the collection as a whole and typify precisely the sophisticated, knowledgeable, idiosyncratic aesthetic of the Messel/Rosse family over six generations. Each garment reminded us of different moments and events in the life of this remarkable family and in doing so confirmed Russell Belk's view that 'after a lifetime of collecting, the objects may be memory cues for a wealth of experiences.'[3]

Certainly this family, like all others, was subject to its own tensions and difficulties. Oliver Messel felt that Marion Sambourne had been 'severe in bringing up my mother'.[4] John Gielgud, whose father was Leonard's junior business partner, described Maud as an 'extremely gentle and kind' but also 'detected a somewhat steely character which occasionally emerged from beneath her gracious exterior', adding that she manipulated 'charm with unexpected firmness'.[5] Maud was certainly indulged by her devoted and wealthy husband.

Anne's letters and notes reveal a patronising social attitude towards those who worked for her, constantly referring to the men as 'little'; examples include 'the little footman' of her childhood at Lancaster Gate and 'the little Oriental men … who came to show [Leonard] fans that he … desired to obtain'.[6] Men whose erudition she admired were, however, immediately and effusively called 'Dear', such as the connoisseur

above Plate 80 Detail of Chinese ceremonial vest.

below Plate 81 Badge of office on Chinese ceremonial vest.

Plate 79 Evening dress by Irene Gilbert, c.1960.

nicknamed 'Dear Numph' who took Oliver Messel to see silk being woven in Spitalfields[7] and 'Dearest John', on her letters to John Morley, Director of the Royal Pavilion in the 1980s. The theatre designer R. Myerscough-Walker, in throwing a light on Oliver Messel's character, has also provided a reflection on his sister, Anne's:

> He comes from a very well known and old family and his social aura is one concerned with society; that is to say the so-called 'Society Set' of the English upper class. … It also makes it surprising that a person of this upbringing should be so industrious … he is one of the most hard-working and meticulous men I have known. Messel is no snob but he appears very far removed from the executants with whom he works.[8]

As to Anne, there is little doubt, as Nicholson confirms, that she could also be 'intransigent' when she felt crossed.[9]

Our focus here has neglected analysis of the distinguished male Messel and Rosse family lines. There is even a related collection of male dress, including eighteenth-century Masonic robes, a range of military and civic uniforms, including those of Leonard, as well as the Hon. Desmond Parson's Chinese robes and a collection of Lord Snowdon's fashionable clothing of the 1960s, donated to Brighton Museum in the 1980s.

It is clear that the passions and committed interests of the men and the women of this family passed down through the generations. Leonard was deeply conscious of his heritage and kept in touch with Irene Messel, the last direct relative connected to his father's German Jewish family. She was the daughter of the architect Alfred Messel, Leonard's uncle, who died in 1909. Nicholson writes that Leonard sent funds to rescue Irene and her husband from Germany[10] as Nazi anti-Semitic policies threatened their lives in the late 1930s.

Leonard and Maud passed on their specific aesthetic 'eye' to Anne and her brother, Oliver Messel.[11] His style, especially his imaginative and rich recreations of the eighteenth century, became so famous and recognisable in the 1930s-50s period, that in the theatre world the terms 'Messelated' or 'Messelian' were used to describe his 'look'. Sir Roy Strong, Director of the V&A, commented that he was 'of course a romantic of the Rex Whistler generation… [his] work always had that slightly unreal, transparent, bleached-out effect, as though we were being presented with an hallucination from an earlier century'.[12]

Neither Anne nor her brother was interested in the contemporary art of their period. Messel's sets and costume designs were based on his skilful talents as a painter and a hands-on maker, fused with a profound

Plate 82 Anna, Lady Oxmantown's wedding dress, 2004.

knowledge of dress and decorative arts history, passed on by his parents. He may well have used the surviving family clothes and photographs in this collection as a source of inspiration, including the Lord Carnarvon suit, the Chinese garments and Marion's dresses of the 1870s and '80s. A design for 'Gigi in her ball gown' for a stage version of *Gigi*, which toured America in 1973, is in fact a sketch of his mother Maud, exactly reminiscent of photographs of her taken in 1902–05.[13] Anne Rosse shared her brother's sense of decor and design, described aptly by Roger Pinkham as 'a playfulness and whimsicality purveyed with charm and taste.'[14]

The creative 'eye' passes on again, to Lady Rosse's son, Lord Snowdon, a world renowned photographer by the late 1950s and, again, in turn, to his daughter, Lady Sarah Chatto, an established artist, who graduated from the Royal College of Art, London. Her brother, David, Viscount Linley, a furniture designer-maker, has established his own successful interior-design company *Linley*, in London's Pimlico, which produces contemporary furniture to commission.

William Brendan, the 7th Earl of Rosse and Alison, Lady Rosse, took over responsibility for Birr Castle in 1979, by which time both the castle and the gardens were run down. Lord Rosse worked for many years for the United Nations, with postings to Dahomey, Ghana, Iran, Bangladesh and Algeria.[15] For years, the great telescope, *The Leviathan*, lay dismantled and decaying until, with Irish government and other funding support, he succeeded in resurrecting it in 1997. Lord and Lady Rosse also developed the new Galleries of Discovery in Birr Castle Demense. Oisin Deery writes that when they inherited the estate the horticultural staff were down from sixteen to six and 'the gardens had run down'. As an indication of the high cultural value placed nationally on this estate, the Irish government also provided funding support for the renewal of the gardens from their 'Great Gardens of Ireland Restoration Programme'.[16]

Lady Rosse, *née* Alison, Cooke-Hurle, of Startforth Hall, Barnard Castle, County Durham, married William Brendan, Lord Oxmantown, in 1966 and shares with Marion, Maud and Anne an elegant and stylish sense of fashion. She wore a bright red mini dress on her honeymoon and patronised Irish designers (Appendix 281). The couple have three children, Laurence Patrick, Lord Oxmantown, Lady Alicia and the Hon. Michael Parsons. Lord Oxmantown married Anna Lin in 2004, and thus, after generations of deep interest in Chinese culture, the family will absorb its very own Chinese heritage. For their wedding in China in the summer of 2004, Anna Lin wore a striking contemporary interpretation of a traditional Chinese wedding dress, made by Guyu, to Anna's design. It is strapless, in the correct auspicious colour of red, with a huge flying phoenix embroidered in coloured silks. This flows down the full length of the front of the dress from bodice to hem (Plate 82). She designed two others dresses for the occasion, and for her Irish blessing she designed a Victorian Gothick-styled gown, in keeping with Birr Castle, in white silk

trimmed with pearls (Appendix 283). These form the final wedding dresses in the collection (so far).

We are all linked to each layer of our family's past, one to the other, generation by generation. Few of us, however, retain six generations of family clothing to remind us of our heritage. In this case the line runs from the c.1870 moiré silk dress of Marion Sambourne (Appendix 3) to Anna Lin's wedding dress, 2004. In 1993, the American scholar Anne Smart Martin wrote that 'material objects matter because they are complex, symbolic bundles of social, cultural and individual meanings fused onto something we can touch, see and own.'[17] This view is entirely confirmed by the existence of the Messel Dress Collection.

Through a close focus on the design, making, consumption and survival of these precious garments and archives, we have sought to touch on the respect and love each generation of this family had, and has, for the one before. Maud's pet name for her father, right through her adult life, was 'Darling Dad'. Anne wrote of her 'wonderful father'[18] and that her mother, Maud, was 'enormously clever and refined … This beautiful mother of ours was the most romantic person in the world.'[19] Lord Rosse today remembers his grandmother, Maud, very fondly.

Each generation was (and is) deeply conscious of the cultural worth of their family art and artefact collections. This awareness would be expected to embrace the heritage of a great family home, such as Birr, with its fine interiors and decorative arts collection. What was far more unusual was the far-sighted and successful fight conducted by Anne, Countess of Rosse and her husband to conserve the Georgian architectural heritage of England and Ireland, and later, the Victorian interiors of Linley Sambourne House itself. We have also highlighted Anne's role in the 1930s in actively helping to develop the extraordinary talent of the couturier, Charles James, and the creativity of Irish fashion designers. Even rarer than all of this, however, has been (again through Anne Rosse), the preservation of these generations of clothes. That is both precious and fortuitous.

It is, of course, not unusual for women to value their best clothes and to hesitate for years before discarding them. Whilst we have seen that Marion was forced to sell off some of hers, Maud and Anne, as our Appendix makes clear, carried this to extremes, keeping garments from their 'coming-out' years through to their old age. Both were petite (size 8–10) all their lives and thus could, had they wished, have continued to wear these garments. Anne indeed chose to do just this from time to time. Maud began the collection, keeping, storing and treasuring these objects. Anne became the second collector, a conscious preserver of her family heritage.

Maud and Leonard, Anne and Michael, the 6th Earl of Rosse and today, William Brendan, the 7th Earl of Rosse and his wife, Alison, Lady Rosse, have cherished these clothes with loving care. As we have shown, even as some of these garments decayed, Maud and Anne fully

Plate 83 Maud Messel's going-away hat, 1898.

recognised their power to evoke precious memories – Maud's note pinned to her mother, Marion's 1898 blue silk dress and another note pinned by Anne, to her mother's sprig of flowers: 'White heather from Maud's wedding bouquet, April 8th 1898.' Since Maud's death in 1960, her heliotrope going away outfit of 1898 with its lilac trimmed, pink straw hat, trimmed at the back with dove's wings (Plate 83) has been the one outfit that the family has loved above all. Today, although the dress is sadly damaged, this romantic honeymoon hat remains in perfect condition and today evokes perfectly Maud's elegant, romantic sense of style.

Marion, Maud and Anne – a style comparison

The women of this family were well informed about the specific periods of the arts that interested them. Their use of this knowledge, typically of their gender, period and social positions, was inevitably focused on private and civic 'feminine' activities. Their talents were directed to their homes and gardens, to the upbringing of their children, as well as, in the case of Maud and Anne, on the expected range of local and civic duties.

Marion, Maud and Anne were all fully aware that their public appearances were assessed critically and had to be carefully composed and controlled. All knew the correct rules of sartorial etiquette suitable to their specific place in society, though Maud had to learn upper-middle/upper-class rules and Anne had to learn Court regulations once she became a Countess.

Marion Sambourne was the one conventional fashion dresser of the three. Her daughter Maud was able to dress far more expensively and was also the most prettily romantic of the three, whilst Marion's grand-daughter Anne, Countess of Rosse, was the most elegant. Marion's status in London society was firmly middle class, though well connected to the fine arts world. She chose not to dress in the extreme aesthetic style preferred by the wives of many artists of her generations. Rather, she wore carefully selected etiquette-correct, middle-of-the-road conventional styles. The Sambournes' financial position made her worry about the cost of her clothing. She was therefore obliged to use modestly priced private dressmakers, to shop in department stores (albeit elegant ones), to re-work her clothes and even to sell off unwanted garments to a second clothes dealer. What is sad to read from her own diaries is how often she was stressed both by fashion-buying anxieties and a lack of personal confidence about her appearance, characteristics that certainly did not trouble either her daughter or granddaughter. Marion's concerns over achieving a properly correct appearance and over her preparations to launch her daughter into society were repeated in the homes of very many middle-class women of her day.

As to Maud and Anne, what differentiates them from more conventional women of their respective periods, is that both so very consciously and successfully created their own highly individual self-images, their own personal style even for fancy-dress occasions. Anne was sufficiently interested to keep two large scrap books consisting solely of fashion reports on her clothes in the 1930s. These, as discussed earlier, always noted Anne's elegant individuality, often commenting on her dressmaking expertise. Thus the fashion reported for the *London Evening News* noted on 1 February, 1931, that 'In her leisure she makes clothes as another woman might paint portraits … I know no-one smarter or more individual in her dress.'[20]

Marion, Maud and Anne also differed from many women of their social circles in that they were all skilled and devoted dressmakers and embroiderers, one generation teaching the next. All three used private dressmakers, but whereas Marion was clearly intimidated by some of hers, both Maud and Anne had the confidence to discuss and plan designs with their couturiers. All couture clients do this to some extent but Maud and Anne insisted on specific, highly personal and symbolic inclusions – such as the piece of an eighteenth-century-man's waistcoat, (Plate 21), or blue scarab fastenings (Plate 86) or 'ammonite' silver buttons (Plate 84).

Plate 84 Button on a Madam Rosse jacket, c.1907.

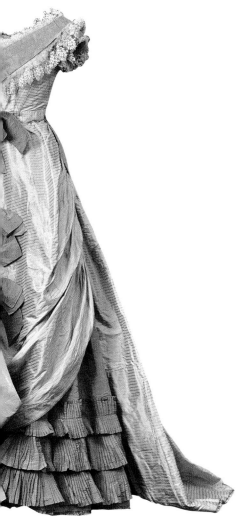

Plate 85 Dress by Charles James, 1936 (left); dress by S.A. Brooking, c.1874 (right).

Plate 86 Scarab fastening on Maud Messel's going-away outfit, 1898.

Unlike Marion, both Maud and Anne also had the courage to wear unusual and striking garments, such as Maud's beautiful but curious brick-red cotton muslin summer dress of about 1905 (Plate 26), with its hand-painted floral decoration and Anne's dramatic, circular, full-length, blue velvet 'medieval' cloak from the mid-to-late 1930s, with its heavy gold collar and tassel (Plate 70). Furthermore, Maud and Anne altered their couture clothes, adding their own idiosyncratic touches, such as the Nymans embroidery crookedly placed on the front of Maud's 1906–08 *Mascotte* dress (Plate 38) and Anne's addition of coloured glass bead embroidery to her 1920s water-lily print chiffon dress (Plate 51). The Countess of Rosse continued to make such additions all her life. In her old age, she was still smoking Turkish cigarettes and drinking Dubonnet and champagne. She was also tempted by the fashionable but cheap styles available at C&A, turning these into unique dresses entirely in her own style, as Lord Snowdon remembered.[21]

Marion, Maud and Anne unusually also wore dresses they had made themselves both for formal and fancy-dress occasions. All made dresses for their daughters. Marion stitched a pink silk 'coming-out' dress for Maud in 1893, whilst Anne made her daughter Susan's white satin wedding dress of 1950 (Appendix 280), and in 1953 makes her daughter a ravishing, yellow silk evening dress for a late invitation to Buckingham Palace the next evening (Plate 74).

Maud and Anne both clearly enjoyed garments which carried refined touches of the 'aesthetic', but only just enough to make them distinctive, in a sophisticated and elegant manner. Whilst Marion's clothes were pretty, smart but conventional, Maud's style was soft and quaintly picturesque although always, always fashionable. Anne was braver than both in departing from the expected. Her confidence in dressing increased through her life as a result of her dress-making training, her practical design work with her brother in the 1920s and '30s and, above all, through her work with Charles James.

It is our belief, as discussed in Chapter 7, that her friendship with Charles James may have had a powerful influence on the development of his work. James visited her in Linley Sambourne House in the early-to-mid-1930s, and, as Victoria Messel comments in her Preface to this book, it was there that the family's dresses of the 1870s and '80s were stored. So Anne could well have shown him Marion's 1874 dress in Linley Sambourne House. Certainly there is a strong shape, colour and even structural parallel between the pink, amber and pale blue evening dress by James, of 1936 (with its back lacing and its curiously shaped skirt) and Marion's *Brooking* costume of about 1874. This is made in the exact same shades of pink and amber, with a similar silhouette and looped skirt drapery and with the very same lacing at the centre back (Plate 85).

It is evident that neither Marion nor Maud nor Anne ever let go of their concern over their appearance, though for Maud, confined as she was to a wheelchair, this was harder in her old age. Anne's appearance

by contrast became more and more striking as she became older. The Countess of Rosse was determined to remain elegant in her later years when she was already frail and her sight was failing. In 1977, when she was seventy five, Sir Roy Strong, by then Director of the V&A, described her at a reception held for Harold Acton by Princess Margaret and Lord Snowdon 'in her usual low cut dress with a slit hemline and manacled in diamond stars.'[22] He met her again in 1982 when she was eighty, at a French Embassy 'fête for gardeners, in honour of the Chelsea Flower Show'. He described her then as 'a miracle at some vast age wearing a dress out of Beaton's Ascot scene of black slashed over white, twinkling with jewels.'[23]

Dispersal of homes

Anne was still regularly using 18 Stafford Terrace for receptions and meetings into the 1970s. In April of 1970, Roy Strong noted in his diary on 16 April, 1970: 'The real event of the day was the Rosses' party for Harold Acton in honour of his new book *More Memoirs of an Aesthete*. No 18 Stafford Terrace must be one of the best surviving domestic interiors from the 1880s in London.' More sadly, the house was used again in November 1978, after the Thanksgiving Service in memory of Oliver Messel at St Martin-in-the-Fields. Strong commented that 'Anne Rosse looked very drawn in black fur hat and veils.'[24]

Anne's husband died just one year later and Reena Suleman comments that after this 'Anne sold the house to the Greater London Council with the proviso that it would be opened to the public as a museum and remain unaltered.' This has indeed miraculously been the case and now this fascinating house is the responsibility of the Royal Borough of Kensington and Chelsea.

The fate of Nymans was, as we have seen, more complex. Leonard and Maud never returned to live in the house after the trauma of its destruction and the loss of so much of Leonard's collection in the 1947 fire, though he visited his gardens regularly. Once it was clear that Leonard and Maud could no longer live there, careful inventories were commissioned from specialists[25] and Maud went through her own and her mother's surviving clothes, adding her little notes here and there, as we have seen.

In 1958, six years after Leonard's death, the Lancaster Gate house was and sold and its contents and furniture were dispersed to Nymans, Birr and some to the Old House in the grounds at Nymans, which Leonard had given to Antony Armstrong-Jones in 1952. Originally known as Little Bletchley's, this dates from the mid-seventeenth century.[26] Sales at Sotheby's followed in October and November of 1963 and at Christie's in 1971.

Leonard had bequeathed Nymans to the National Trust in 1949 in lieu

Plate 87 Anne, Countess of Rosse at Nymans.

of death duties, on the condition that Maud or one of the children had the right to occupy the house. After his death, the gardens thus became one the first in the country to pass into the care of the Trust. Michael had been elected on to its Council the year before. Maud's role as advisor, however, proved problematic. Nicholson writes that her 'Edwardian attitudes, her dreamy voice and unfinished sentences, quite nonplussed outsiders who tried to apply modern ideas to the administration of a run-down estate' and so negotiations passed into the capable hands of Anne and Michael Rosse.[27]

After Michael's death in 1979, alterations were made to allow Anne to live in the house[28] and here she spent her last widowed years until her death in 1992. Her secretary, Daphne Dengate, recalled that 'I went to see her every morning and to do anything she wanted as I used to do for her mother, though they were very different in character.' Miss Dengate felt that Anne was 'very lonely' at first, but that she 'was brave and occupied herself with the garden of which she was the Director.'[29] It was in this period that the Countess of Rosse placed large amounts of the family dress collection at the Brighton Museum for safe keeping, and removed the rest to Birr Castle. She struggled with her health in her last years, facing hip-replacement surgery and dealing with her deteriorating sight (Plate 87).

After the death of the Countess of Rosse in 1992, surviving sections of the house on the ground floor were altered, in a successful attempt to create rooms which would give the visiting public an idea of the old atmosphere of the house (Plate 88). In 1994, a final auction of unwanted items from Nymans, including many household textiles, was organised by Christie's, with some items finding their way on to the second-hand textiles market in Brighton. Victoria Messel organised this sale, ensuring that none of the clothes or textiles significantly related to the history of the family was sold. Thus the National Trust took care of the precious boxes of Nymans Needlework Guild embroideries, many of Maud's antique textiles and the eighteenth-century dress and suit. The most recent sale of artefacts related directly to Nymans was held in 2002. A Sotheby's press release stated that furniture, silver and other artefacts from the Old House were to be sold on 30 September, including furniture collected by the Messels – a Charles I oak tester bed, for example, which may have been Maud's, a George III carved mahogany and a large selection of silver and Sheffield silver plate from the late sixteenth to the nineteenth century.

Plate 88 Nymans interior.

Survival – homes and gardens

As for 18, Stafford Terrace, through the far-sightedness and determination of Anne, Countess of Rosse, this house provides an original memory of the taste of the second generation of this family. Caught today in the hustle and bustle of London, just off Kensington High Street, this house, open today to all of us, retains the late, wonderfully cluttered, nineteenth-century interior, created by Anne's grandparents, Linley and Marion Sambourne. Reena Suleman writes that 'little valued in the 1950s [it is] now recognised as a national treasure of moderated English arts and craft taste of the late 19th century.'

As a direct result of the marriage of Anne and Michael, the gardens at Birr and Nymans also flourish today, including the cross-bred magnolias established there by Ludwig in 1905. They are now are cared for by David Masters, the head gardener, who worked with Anne Rosse before she died. In spring 2005, a rhododendron reared in the gardens won Nymans another prize from the Royal Horticultural Society.

What has become clear throughout this research is that from the 1850s this extended family was, and is, profoundly absorbed by gardens, trees and plants. The last hybrids named after members of the family are the *Magnolia* 'Michael Rosse', developed in 1968, 'with large flowers of soft purple pink,' in 1970, the *Magnolia* 'Anne Rosse' of 1973, with pink buds opening as white flowers and the *Lonicera* 'Michael Rosse' (Plates 89 & 90), which won an award in 1982.[30] Others trees and shrubs, including rhododendrons, bear the Rosse and Nymans names. Oisin Deery comments that Lord and Lady Rosse today 'have also collected seeds and introduced plants from all over the world including Nepal, Tibet and Western China.'[31] As Pearce believes, 'collecting is not the same as ordinary consumer behaviour.' Collecting has been termed a 'positive addition … a blessed obsession'.[32]

Plate 89 *Magnolia* 'Michael Rosse'.

Plate 90 *Magnolia* 'Anne Rosse'.

Conclusion

There is another level on which the gardens operate. They remain constantly in the mind's eye of the family and were, and are, both an economic and creative challenge as well as a source of intense pleasure. The present Lord Rosse, commenting on the planned juxtaposition of red, green and purple dresses in our exhibition, noted immediately that these colours combined to form the colours of fuchsias. In troubled times both the gardens and the habit of collecting became a comfort and a solace. Thus in 1947, after the traumatising shock of the loss of Nymans, Leonard, with encouragement from the family, took up again his 'blessed obsession'. The little late eighteenth-century miniature by Samuel Cotes of Elizabeth Linley was purchased, as well as the gorgeous 'Lord Carnarvon' 1775–80 embroidered suit (Plate 45, Fig. 27) and some replacement

jewellery for Maud, including an early Victorian rose diamond brooch from Heming and Co. Conduit Street.[33] After the tragic death of the young artist, Robert Brough, in January 1905, Maud tried to bring solace to her mother with thoughts of forthcoming spring garden growth. On a cold January day, she wrote to her mother, who was in London, from Balcombe House in Sussex:

> This beautiful air is a luxury after the stuffy atmosphere of London and the garden is full of promise for the Spring. Kiss my darling Dad for me and tell him how truly I feel for him on Mr Brough's death. These sad times fall not lightly upon his dear loving nature. With all my love to you, my sweet mother.[34]

All of this is directly reflected in the dress collection. It is seen, for example, in Maud's choice in 1898 of her lilac strewn hat, in the care with which Oliver Messel designed and made the pretty floral wedding wreath for his niece, Susan Armstrong-Jones, in 1950 (Plate 91). It is, above all, apparent in the Countess of Rosse's use of floral motifs on so many her clothes. At first this took the form of pretty prints in her mid-to-late 1920s (Plate 51), but by the late 1940s and into the 1960s, bright, bolder floral prints, appliqués and brocades were the mainstay of her wardrobe, typified by the Irene Gilbert's carnation dress. It is clear in the choice of the deep pink artificial camellia that Lady Rosse sewed on her daughter's home-made, yellow dress to wear at Buckingham Palace in 1953, the very same shade as the camellias found in the gardens at Nymans and Birr on a spring day (Plate 74). It is as if Lady Rosse cannot bear to abandon the flowers outside in her garden but brings them into her indoor life through her garments, and indeed, through her flower arrangements.

This study has sought to interpret these garments as precious holders of the Sambourne-Messel-Rosse family memory, heritage and character, set within each generation's differing economic circumstances, social space and period style. These garments relate intimately to the family passion for the decorative arts, for fashion, for dressing up and for their great gardens. From the 1870s onwards, the women of this extended family, Marion, Maud, Anne, Susan, Alison and today, Anna, were and are able to turn their social obligations to dress correctly into clear, personal style statements. Further, the survival of this collection is also a testament to their wider understanding of the need to conserve the material goods of the historic past.

It has been our intent, through exploring the coded sartorial messages that lie within these remarkable clothes, to raise a general awareness of the cultural value of clothing – all clothing. Our 'story' here is more than a eulogy to these beautiful garments and the family associated with them, or even a grateful thanks for the preservation of these clothes. We have sought to demonstrate through this case study that the application of a

Plate 91 Susan, Viscountess de Vesci's wedding wreath by Oliver Messel, 1950.

close, garment-focused study of surviving clothes can help us touch the memories, emotions, aspirations and sensitivities of their owners, characteristics which drive the world along and yet which are so often left out of historical study and museum interpretations.

[1] Birr Castle archives, at the Public Record Office of Northern Ireland, contain papers derived from the Yorkshire marriages of the 3rd, 4th and 5th Earls (in 1836, 1870 and 1905 respectively) and hence papers from 1682–1987, of the Hawke family, about the estate at Womersley.

[2] Judith Rutherford and Jackie Menzies, 'Celestial Silks, Chinese Religious and Court Textiles', Art Gallery of New South Wales, Sydney, 2004, pp. 68, 87 and 89. With thanks to Hannah and Noah Taylor.

[3] Russell W. Belk, *Collecting in a Consumer Society*, Routledge, London, 1995, p. 151.

[4] Castle Charles, *Oliver Messel: A biography,* Thames and Hudson, London, 1986, p. 26.

[5] Ibid., pp. 7–8.

[6] Anne Rosse, 'Leonard Messel, The Collector and the Man 1872–1953', article for the Fan Circle. Undated, probably mid-1980s, Birr Archives.

[7] Castle Charles, *op. cit.*, 1986, p. 30.

[8] Roger Pinkham (ed.), *Oliver Messel*, V&A, London, 1983, p. 34.

[9] Shirley Nicholson, *op. cit.*, p. 132.

[10] Ibid., p. 98.

[11] See Roger Pinkham, *Oliver Messel.*

[12] Ibid., p. 8.

[13] Ibid., fig. 94 and compare to photographs of Maud in the 1898–1905 period at Nymans Archive and Sambourne Family Archive.

[14] Ibid. p. 17.

[15] Sally Shaw, 'Childhood glimpses at Birr Castle', *Ireland of the Welcomes*, vol. 36, no. 2 March – April 1987.

[16] Oisin Deery, a compact History of Birr, Tama Books, Dublin, 2001, p. 105.

[17] Ann Smart Martin, 'Makers, Buyers and Users, Consumerism as a Material Cultural Framework', *Winterthur Portfolio*, vol. 28, nos. 2/4, Summer/Autumn, 1993, pp. 141–57.

[18] Anne Rosse, 'Leonard Messel, The Collector and the Man 1872–1953'.

[19] Charles Castle, *op. cit.*, 1986, pp. 20–25.

[20] Anne Rosse's personal scrapbooks 1930s, Birr Archives.

[21] Robert Byrne, 'Couture for a Countess: Lady Rosse's Wardrobe', *Irish Arts Review Year Book*, 1996, vol. 12, p. 162.

[22] Roy Strong, *The Roy Strong Diaries 1967–1987*, Weidenfeld and Nicholson, London, 1997, entry for 28 November 1977, p. 205; entry for 20 May 1982, p. 318.

[23] Ibid., entry for 16 April 1970, referring to his designs for the film, *My Fair Lady*, pp. 64–65.

[24] Ibid., entry for 9 November 1978, p. 229.

[25] These are to be found in the Nymans Archives.

[26] Inventories were made of the contents of this house by Clifford Smith in 1949. (See National Art Library, V&A, London, Press mark 86.W.113.

[27] Shirley Nicholson, *op. cit.*, p. 119.

[28] Ibid. see chapter 10.

[29] 'The Memoirs of Daphne Dengate', unprovenanced typed script, c. 2004. Village Archives, Staplefield.

[30] Shirley Nicholson, *op. cit.*, pp. 150, 139.

[31] Deery, *op. cit.*, 2001, p. 104.

[32] Susan Pearce, *On Collecting*, Routledge, London, 1995, p. 148.

[33] Nymas Archives, Box 54, letter of 22 July 1948.

[34] Letter from Maud Messel to her mother Marion in London, dated 22 January 1905, Nymans Archives.

Appendix

Eleanor Thompson

This appendix documents the clothes worn by the female members of the family across all the locations in which they are stored: Brighton Museum & Art Gallery, Birr Castle, Co. Offaly Ireland and Nymans House in West Sussex. Those objects numbered CT004001 – CT004151 and CT004370 are on long-term loan to Brighton Museum from the estate of Anne, Countess of Rosse, made available courtesy of the Earl of Rosse, the Earl of Snowdon, the Hon Martin Parsons and Victoria Messel, those numbered CT004152 – CT004369 are on loan to the Museum from The Royal Borough of Kensington and Chelsea; Linley Sambourne House Museum.

There is another, equally important collection of men's wear at Brighton and Birr which encompasses civil, military and court uniforms, Masonic robes, special occasion wear and fancy dress.

First Generation:
Mary Anne Herapath (née Walker)

Mourning Bodices

1. *Madame Elphick, c.1884:*
Crape black woollen cloth with glass beads.
Brighton, CT004041.

2. *Mrs. J. J. Carnley, c.1884–85:*
Black silk brocade with black beads.
Brighton, CT004042.

Second Generation:
Marion Sambourne (née Herapath)

Dresses: Day and Evening

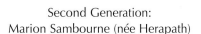

3. *c.1870:*
Purple moiré silk, skirt, evening bodice and day jacket trimmed with Maltese lace.
Birr.

4. *c.1874:*
Day skirt and jacket of brown and white silk.
Birr.

5. *S. A. Brooking, c.1874:*
Skirt, day bodice and evening bodice of pink and amber satin.
Birr.

6. *c.1885:*
Bodice and skirt of dark green silk velvet and silk.
Brighton, CT004271.

7. *c.1895:*
Light brown, green and purple silk.
Worn by Marion Sambourne or Maud Messel.
Birr.

Daywear: Jacket

8. *c.1900–1910:*
Brown beaver fur, lined with cream-coloured satin.
Brighton, CT004217.

Daywear: Blouses

9. *c.1900–1905:*
Three of white cotton lace, embroidered in white thread 'M. Sambourne'.
Brighton, CT004241, CT004242, CT004244.

10. *c.1900–1905:*
Cream-coloured wool and lace.
Brighton, CT004246.
Worn by Marion Sambourne or Maud Messel.

11. *1900–05:*
Cream-coloured silk with cotton lace.
Brighton, CT004262.
Worn by Marion Sambourne or Maud Messel.

12. *c.1900–1910:*
Three white cotton lace.
Brighton, CT004243, CT004245, CT004248.
Worn by Marion Sambourne or Maud Messel.

13. *c.1905:*
Light pink satin, with lace and ribbon.
Brighton, CT004247.
Worn by Marion Sambourne or Maud Messel.

14. *Debenham & Freebody, c. 1912–14:*
White silk.
Brighton, CT004258.
Worn by Marion Sambourne or Maud Messel.

Special Occasion Clothing

15. *Dress, Sarah Fullerton Monteith Young, 1898:*
Bodice, skirt and belt of blue, cream-coloured and gold silk.
Brighton, CT004315.
Worn at Marion's daughter Maud's wedding to Leonard Messel 1898.

Mourning Clothing

16. *Skirts, c.1900–1910*
Six of black silk and velvet.
Brighton, CT004164, CT004172, CT004174, CT004175, CT004204, CT004311.
Worn by Marion Sambourne or Maud Messel.

17. *Outfit, c.1897:*
Jacket, bodice and skirt of black silk velvet with astrakhan and jet buttons.
Brighton, CT004227.

18. *Suit, c.1910–1912:*
Bodice and skirt of black velvet with lace.
Brighton. CT004268.

19. *Suit, Marshall & Snelgrove, c.1912–14:*
Jacket and skirt of black cotton and satin.
Brighton, CT004264.

20. *Suit, c.1914:*
Jacket and skirt of black linen with braid.
Brighton, CT004265.

21. *Bodice, c.1910:*
Black silk and chiffon.
Brighton, CT004165

22. *Bag, c.1910:*
Black leather with black beads, lined
with black silk and cream-coloured kid
leather, contains mirror CT004283 and
powder puff CT004284.
Brighton, CT004282.

See also appendix 106–07.

Nightwear and underwear

23. *Nightgowns, c.1900–1910:*
Three white cotton with lace,
embroidered 'M. Sambourne'.
Brighton, CT004238 – CT004240.

24. *Nightgown, c.1900–1910:*
Cream-coloured wool flannel with
lace, embroidered 'M A S'.
Brighton, CT004316.

25. *Chemises, c.1900–1910*
Five white cotton, embroidered 'M
Sambourne'.
Brighton, CT004253 – CT004256,
CT004366.

26. *Camisoles, c.1900–1910:*
Five white cotton lace with ribbon,
embroidered 'S'.
Brighton, CT004259 – CT004261.
CT004274, CT004277.

Miscellaneous items

27. *Apron, c.1900–1910:*
White cotton, embroidered 'S'.
Brighton, CT004257.

28. *Cushion Covers, c.1870s–1914*
White cotton and white silk,
embroidered 'M S' and 'M.
Sambourne'.
Brighton, CT004273, CT004278.

29. *Box of dressmaking materials,*
1880s–1914.
Brighton.

See also appendix 156–57.

Third Generation: Maud Messel (née Sambourne)

30. *Baby clothes, c.1875:*
Thirty-five white cotton baby dresses,
vests, petticoats and shirts.
Brighton, CT004115 – CT004149.
Worn by Maud and Roy Sambourne

Daywear: Dresses

31. *Sarah Fullerton Monteith Young,*
c.1902–05:
Bodice and skirt of cream-coloured
muslin, with orange satin ribbon and
buckle set with pink stones.
Brighton, CT004037.

32. *c.1905:*
Bodice, skirt and belt of red chiffon,
hand-painted Greco-Turkish rose and
leaf motif outlined in gold.
Brighton, CT004021.

33. *Mascotte, c.1906–08:*
Bodice and skirt of brown velvet, silk
chiffon, with brown glass beads and
appliquéd motif.
Brighton, CT004216.

34. *Frederique, c.1910:*
Cream-coloured gauze.
Brighton, CT004016.

35. *c.1912:*
Light grey silk crêpe.
Brighton, CT004048.

36. *Reville & Rossiter, c.1915–20:*
Brown silk-backed wool crêpe with moulded buttons, brown satin under dress.
Brighton, CT004058.

Daywear: Walking Costumes

37. *c.1896–89:*
Skirt and jacket of green wool twill, with metal 'buttons', lined in cream-coloured and black silk with small pink flowers. Matching green silk blouse by Mme Josephine Gilli.
Brighton, CT004055.

38. *Madame Hayward, c.1902–05*
Skirt: Grey silk crepon, grey glacé silk underskirt, grey satin sash.
Bolero Jacket: Grey silk crêpon with blue silk braid, lined in grey satin.
Blouse: White chiffon with cream-coloured lace and purple satin ribbon.
Brighton, CT004025.

39. *c.1905:*
Skirt and jacket of grey wool tweed.
Brighton, CT004237.

40. *c.1907–09:*
Skirt and jacket of grey marled wool crêpe with black cord and white linen.
Brighton, CT004228.

41. *Sarah Fullerton Monteith Young, c.1909–10*
Dress: Light green wool flannel with cream-coloured lace, white and gold silk braid and gold metallic buckles set with jade stones, cream-coloured silk underskirt, cream-coloured lace plastron front.
Jacket: Light green wool flannel with lace and beige silk lining.
Brighton, CT004024.

42. *Lucile, c.1912–13:*
Skirt and jacket of dark brown wool face cloth, collar and cuffs of moleskin, lined with light brown satin.
Brighton, CT004027.

43. *c.1915–20:*
Dress and jacket of brown silk georgette, with glass beads and swansdown.
Brighton, CT004018.

44. *c.1915–20:*
Jacket: Brown wool mix with grey-brown fur and brown, black and white twill.
Overdress: Brown chiffon and brown, black and white twill.
Underdress: Light brown silk and brown wool.
Brighton, CT004028.

Daywear: Jackets

45. *Madam Ross, c.1907:*
Black wool with astrakhan, black braid and metal buttons, lined in cream-coloured satin.
Brighton, CT004229.

46. *Samson, c.1907:*
Grey brushed wool tweed, with black, cream-coloured and brown braid.
Brighton, CT004236.

Daywear: Blouses

47. *1900–05:*
Cream-coloured net with gold thread and gold tissue covered buttons.
Brighton, CT004249.

48. *F. T. L Wilson, 1900–1905:*
Cream-coloured lace and net.
Brighton, CT004251.

49. *c.1910:*
Two of cream-coloured lace with silk ribbon.
Brighton, CT004017, CT004231.

50. *c. 1900–1920:*
Box of mixed blouses.
Birr.
See also appendix 10–14

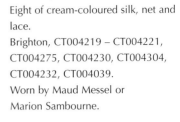

51. *Skirts, c.1900–1910:*
Eight of cream-coloured silk, net and lace.
Brighton, CT004219 – CT004221, CT004275, CT004230, CT004304, CT004232, CT004039.
Worn by Maud Messel or Marion Sambourne.

Teagowns

52. *Reville & Rossiter, c.1900–1910:*
Light green silk corduroy, with yellow and green braid, lined with brown satin.
Brighton, CT004020.

53. *Tea Gown or Maternity Dress, c.1902:*
Lilac crêpe, black velvet with cream-coloured lace.
Brighton, CT004218.

54. *c.1905–10:*
Green glacé silk, cream-coloured bobbin lace, silver and gold thread appliquéd motifs with pink and green glass gemstones.
Brighton, CT004022.

55. *1910:*
Pink silk with cream-coloured cotton collar, lined with cream-coloured wool.
Brighton, CT004022.

56. *c.1910–12:*
Purple silk lined in light grey-green silk chiffon, with embroidered braid,
Brighton, CT004001.

Evening Dresses

57. *Russell & Allen, c.1900:*
Bodice and skirt of cream-coloured silk, black net, black velvet ribbon with diamanté buckle.
Brighton, CT004235.

58. *Sarah Fullerton Monteith Young, c.1902–05:*
Bodice and skirt of gold tissue covered with sprigged lace and net, with 'fish scale' sequins, glacé silk lining.
Brighton, CT004038.

59. *Sarah Fullerton Monteith Young, c.1906:*
Dark pink silk, cream-coloured net and lace, with gilt and pink, black chenille thread covered baubles and braid.
Brighton, CT004034.

60. *Sarah Fullerton Monteith Young, c.1906–08:*
Green silk chiffon trimmed with pearls, silver braid, glass beads and Greek key pattern.
Brighton, CT004005.

61. *Sarah Fullerton Monteith Young, c.1907:*
Purple silk velvet, cream-coloured silk under-bodice taken from eighteenth-century man's embroidered waistcoat.
Brighton, CT004015.

62. *Sarah Fullerton Monteith Young, c.1907:*
Cream-coloured silk net, with turquoise and gilt-metal beads, underskirt of white muslin and white silk ribbon bow.
Brighton, CT004023.

63. *c.1907–08:*
Purple velveteen, with glass beads.
Brighton, CT004209.

64. *c.1907–08:*
Cream-coloured glacé silk, with gold tissue braid, beads and pearls
Brighton. CT004004.

65. *Evening or Fancy Dress, c.1908–10:*
Silver-gilt lamé and green silk chiffon, with pearls and glass beads.
Brighton, CT004003.

66. *Evening or Fancy Dress, c.1910:*
Cream-coloured muslin, gold tissue, with gilt braid and seed pearls, lined in red wool.
Brighton, CT004002.

67. *Evening or Fancy Dress, c.1910:*
Black silk and lace, crêpe underskirt,
three belts with appliquéd motifs.
Brighton, CT004051.

68. *Underdress, c.1910:*
Brown silk trimmed with metal thread.
Brighton, CT004275.

69. *Overdress, c.1910:*
Bright pink chiffon, gold thread
drawstring.
Brighton, CT004061.

70. *c. 1911–12:*
Cream-coloured chiffon, net and lace,
trimmed with ermine.
Brighton, CT004047.

71. *Neville, c.1911–13:*
Cream-coloured duchesse satin with
metallic gold thread.
Brighton, CT004049.

72. *Neville, c.1913:*
Ivory silk crêpon damask, gilt tissue
sash and gold flower.
Brighton, CT004030.

73. *Reville, c. 1923:*
Cream-coloured silk lace with gold and
brown glass beads and brown and
cream-coloured ribbon.
Brighton, CT004050.

74. *Dress and coat, c.1930–35:*
Purple and gold georgette lined in
purple satin.
Brighton, CT004046.

See also appendix 7.

Evening bodices

75. *c.1900–1910:*
Dark blue velvet lined with cream-
coloured satin.
Brighton, CT004234.

76. *Madam Ross, c.1907:*
Cream-coloured silk satin with crewel
work and lace.
Brighton, CT004234.

77. *c.1910–12:*
Blue velvet, black satin and net, cream-
coloured chiffon with black beads and
sequins.
Brighton, CT004205.

Outerwear

78. *Cape, c.1896–98:*
Cream-coloured silk with purple satin.
Brighton, C004169.

79. *Evening cape c.1900–1905:*
Blue velvet, with black beads, jet and cream-coloured lace, lined in pale green taffeta.
Brighton, CT004214.

80. *Chinese coat, c.1900–1914:*
Embroidered purple silk, lined in white fur with monkey fur collar.
Brighton. CT004113.

81. *Chinese jacket, c.1890–1910:*
Embroidered yellow silk brocade, lined in red silk.
Brighton. CT004114.

82. *Evening coat, c.1912:*
Black silk lined in purple silk, with gold and silver metal thread.
Brighton, CT004266.

83. *Evening coat, c.1922–24:*
Black, fine, open-weave silk over cream-coloured Shantung silk with rabbit fur.
Brighton, CT004056.

84. *Evening coat, Reville, c.1923:*
Black silk embroidered in cream-coloured thread, fur collar.
Brighton, CT004062.

85. *Evening coat, J. & F. P. Wilson, c.1924:*
Dark red-brown and gilt tissue brocade, collar and cuffs of monkey fur, lined with dark red silk.
Brighton, CT004032.

Special Occasion Clothing

86. *Wedding Outfit, Sarah Fullerton Monteith Young, 1898*
Dress: Cream-coloured satin, with net and lace, pearl, diamond and turquoise buckle.
Underskirt: Cream-coloured silk.
Veil: Cream-coloured net.
Headdress: Circlet of wax blossom buds and flowers, fabric flowers and leaves.
Shoes, Peter Yapp: Cream-coloured satin.
Brighton, CT004033 & CT004111.1-3.
Worn at her wedding to Leonard Messel 1898.

87. *Going-Away Outfit, Sarah Fullerton Monteith Young, 1898*
Dress: Light purple-pink wool face cloth with moleskin, braid and jewelled buckle.
Jacket: Light purple-pink wool face cloth with moleskin and scarab clasp.
Underskirt: Pink glacé silk.
Stockings: Deep pink knitted silk.
Hat, Woollands: Pink straw, with pink lilac, chiffon and a bird's wing.
Birr.

88. *Going-Away Outfit, Sarah Fullerton Monteith Young, 1898*
Bodice: Skirt and sleeveless bolero jacket of light purple silk and fine wool, with silk braid and opal buttons, lined in glacé silk, white muslin belt, worn with hat, appendix 87.
Birr.

89. *Court train, 1908:*
Cream-coloured satin, with pearls,
lined in ivory satin and silver thread.
Brighton, CT004111.4.

Fancy Dress

90. *Dress, 1913:*
Cream-coloured satin, with green and
gilt braid and appliquéd Turkish or
Greek embroidered motifs.
Brighton, CT004029.

91. *Dress and petticoat, c.1780:*
Cream-coloured and pink Spitalfields
silk.
Nymans.

92. *Suit, c.1775–80:*
Jacket, waistcoat and breeches of
brown silk and cream-coloured
embroidered silk.
Nymans.

See also appendix 65–67.

Mourning clothing: Dresses

93. *c.1910:*
Black georgette and white lace.
Brighton, CT004051.

94. *c.1910–12:*
Black taffeta with jet beads.
Brighton, CT004213.

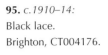

95. *c.1910–14:*
Black lace.
Brighton, CT004176.

96. *Mrs Neville, c.1911–12:*
Black silk, Guipure lace and net, with
jet tassels.
Brighton, CT004170.

97. *Overdress, c.1910–14:*
Black chiffon.
Brighton, CT004181.

98. *Overdress c.1910–14:*
Black net with satin bows.
Brighton, CT004207.

99. *Overdress c.1912–14:*
Black silk chiffon, trimmed with jet
beads.
Brighton, CT004211.

100. *Suit, Reville & Rossiter, 1912:*
Skirt and jacket of black wool with
black fur collar, lined with black satin.
Brighton, CT004026.

Mourning clothing: Bodices

101. *Mrs Neville, c.1905:*
Black wool, cream-coloured satin and net.
Brighton, CT004172.

102. *c.1910:*
Black silk lined in satin.
Brighton, CT004179.

103. *c.1910–14:*
Black Guipure lace over cream-coloured muslin with black beads.
Brighton, CT004206.

104. *c.1910:*
Black silk, velvet and cream-coloured lace.
Brighton, CT004269.

105. *c.1912–14:*
Black velvet, lace and paste beads.
Brighton, CT004168.

106. *Underbodices, c.1910–14*
Three of black silk and satin.
Brighton, CT004180, CT004195, CT004212.
Worn by Marion Sambourne or Maud Messel.

107. *Blouses, c.1910–14*
Two black silk and chiffon.
Brighton, CT004279 and CT004270.
Worn by Marion Sambourne or Maud Messel.

108. *Blouse, Reville & Rossiter, c.1912:*
White muslin with black embroidery.
Brighton, CT004263.

109. *Pantaloons, c.1910–14:*
Black sateen.
Worn by Marion Sambourne or Maud Messel.
Brighton CT004182.

Mourning: outerwear

110. *Evening cape, c.1910:*
Black sateen, with velvet ribbon, braid and sequins, lined with cream-coloured silk.
Brighton, CT004171.

111. *Evening cape, c.1910:*
Black silk taffeta.
Brighton, CT004267.

112. *Coat, c.1910:*
Black corded silk and chiffon.
Brighton, CT004208.

113. *Coat, c.1910:*
Black silk/wool bombazine with blue velvet.
Brighton, CT004163.

Mourning: Hats

114. *F. J. L. Wilson, c.1910:*
Black straw, with black velvet and black feathers.
Brighton, CT004070.

115. *c.1910–12:*
Black velvet with large black ostrich feather and French jet.
Brighton. CT004152.

116. *c.1910–14:*
Black straw with sateen ribbon.
Brighton, CT004066.

117. *Hat trim, Fitzali, c.1910–14:*
Black velvet, silk and lace.
Brighton, CT004157.

118. *c.1912–14:*
Black fur/felt, trimmed with two black magpie wings.
Brighton, CT004155.

119. *c.1914:*
Black velvet with ostrich plumes and black net rosette.
Brighton. CT004154.

120. *Payzway, c.1914–15:*
Purple straw with blue ribbon and felt.
Brighton, CT004067.

See also appendix 16.

Bedjackets

121. *c.1900–1920:*
Black corded silk, cream-coloured lace and net.
Brighton, CT004178.

122. *c.1900–1920:*
Pink silk trimmed with lace.
Brighton, CT004252.

Accessories and Miscellaneous: Furs

123. *Stole & Muff, c.1900–1915:*
Mink lined with cream-coloured silk.
Brighton, CT004222.

124. *Stole & Muff, c.1900–1915:*
Red fur.
Brighton, CT004226.

125. *Hat, c.1905:*
Mink with black and white feather wings.
Brighton, CT004223.

126. *Cape, c.1900–1910:*
Beaver and red fox fur, lined with silk satin.
Brighton, CT004224.

127. *Cape, c.1900–1910:*
Red fur.
Brighton, CT004225.

Hats

128. *c.1905:*
Green crin with green velvet bow, ribbons and plumes of ostrich feathers.
Brighton, CT004151.

129. *F. J. L Wilson, c.1910:*
Grey straw, with grey silk and pink edged ostrich feather.
Brighton, CT004071.

130. *c.1912–14:*
Light brown straw hat, brown chiffon with pink/grey feather wings.
Brighton, CT004203.

Shoes

131. *Peter Yapp, c.1910:*
Gold metallic thread.
Brighton, CT004043.

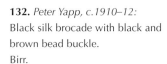

132. *Peter Yapp, c.1910–12:*
Black silk brocade with black and brown bead buckle.
Birr.

133. *Peter Yapp, c.1910–15:*
Brown snakeskin with buckle.
Birr.

134. *Edward Gerret and Co,*
c.1910–15:
Brown suede with brown buckles.
Birr.

135. *1915:*
Dark green velvet with diamanté
buckle.
Brighton, CT004044.

136. *Peter Yapp, c.1915–20:*
Brown leather with gold buckle.
Brighton, CT004063.

137. *Rayne, c.1955:*
Dark blue leather.
Brighton, CT004064.

Bags

138. *c.1905:*
Black velvet.
Brighton, CT004166.

139. *c.1900–1910:*
Green embroidered with initials 'F.S.'
Brighton, CT004280.

140. *c.1916, made by*
Nymans Embroidery Guild:
Cream-coloured embroidered satin
with cream-coloured braid and tassels.
Brighton, CT004281.

141. *c.1911–13, made by*
Nymans Embroidery Guild:
Cream-coloured satin embroidered
with peacocks and fountains.
Brighton, CT004189.

Parasols

142. *Paragon, c.1900–1905:*
Purple and gold shot silk, wooden
stick, carved bamboo handle, metal-
tipped ferrule, with silk pom-poms.
Brighton, CT004348.

143. *S. Fox & Co. Ltd, c.1905:*
Black and white checked silk cover,
white painted wood stick and cut glass
handle.
Brighton, CT004346.

144. *S. Fox & Co. Ltd, c.1910–15:*
White silk with horizontal bands of
black satin, black enamelled wood
stick.
Brighton, CT004347.

145. *Fan:*
Painted silk with white lace, carved
ivory sticks and guards.
Brighton, CT004317.

146. *Buckle, c.1900:*
Metal inset with purple gems.
Brighton, CT004192.

147. *Cameo brooch, c.1900:*
Cream-coloured shell set in brass.
Brighton CT004193.

148. *Travelling jewellery case, c.1900:*
Pink silk with embroidered flowers.
Brighton, CT004194.

149. *Hairpin, c.1900–1905:*
Tortoiseshell.
Brighton, CT004191.

150. *Scarves, c.1900–1914*
Ten of black, cream-coloured, beige
and pink silk.
Brighton, CT004035,
CT004301–CT004303, CT004305,
CT004308 – CT004309, CT004276,
CT004292, CT004313.

151. *Shawl, c.1910–1915:*
Cream-coloured silk printed with
flowers.
Brighton, CT004210.

152. *Feather boas, c.1900–1910*
Black osprey with black satin bow.
Brighton, CT004152.

153. *White swan feather.*
Brighton, C004199.

154. *Belts, c.1910*
Silver thread.
Brighton, CT004059.

155. *Black silk brocade with gold metallic thread fringe.*
Brighton, CT004306.

156. *Sleeves, c.1900–1915:*
Four pairs of net, lace and chiffon.
Brighton, CT004057, CT004288,
CT004350, CT004364.
Worn by Marion Sambourne or
Maud Messel.

157. *Collars and Cuffs, c.1900–1915:*
Assorted bundles of white and black
linen and cotton
Brighton, CT004289, CT004290,
CT004296, CT004298, CT004351.
Worn by Marion Sambourne or
Maud Messel.

158. *Feather trims, c.1900–1915:*
Twelve loose feathers, black and cream
coloured.
Brighton, CT004159 – CT004162,
CT004183 – 88, CT004089,
CT004291.

159. *Sprig of fabric violets:*
Brighton, CT004069.

160. *Collection of bags and table
runners, made by Nymans Embroidery
Guild 1916–1950s*
Linen embroidered with pink, green,
blue and purple threads, embroidery
satin trimmed with gilt tassels.
Nymans.

161. *Collection of Italian Casalguidi
bags, c.1900:*
Linen with raised embroidery.
Nymans.

162. *Chinese Bags:*
Two of embroidered blue and pink and
green and blue.
Nymans.

163. *Collection of threads.*
Nymans

Fourth Generation:
Anne, Countess of Rosse (née Messel)

Daywear: Dresses

164. *Irfé, c.1927:*
White silk crêpe printed with wheat
and floral motif black and white.
Brighton, CT004011.

165. *c.1929:*
Yellow silk chiffon printed with grass
motif in black and grey.
Brighton, CT004012.

166. *c.1929:*
Cream-coloured silk georgette printed
with water lily motif green, white and
yellow on a black ground with silver
thread and yellow glass appliqué
stones,
Brighton, CT004013.

167. *'Spiral Wrap' or 'Taxi' street dress,
Charles James, 1933:*
Black textured linen, metal zipper.
Birr.

168. *'Bali' dress, Charles James, 1935:*
Yellow silk boucle with wine-red linen
sash.
Birr.

169. *'Bali' dress, Charles James, 1935:*
Cream-coloured woven silk with black
sash.
Brighton.

170. *c.1937:*
Navy blue silk printed with pale blue, grey and pink star bursts and 'Jean'.
Birr.

171. *'Snow white' dress Charles James, 1938:*
Navy-blue silk twill with print.
Birr.

172. *Late 1940s:*
Blue silk blouse with appliquéd rose, blue cotton skirt printed with bright pink roses.
Brighton.

173. *Late 1940s:*
Blue silk crêpe printed with flowers and leaves in pink.
Brighton.

174. *Ib Jorgensen:*
Taupe coloured silk crêpe.
Birr.

175. *Ib Jorgensen:*
Sprigged black cotton voile.

176. *1960s–1970s:*
Yellow cotton, printed with red and black floral pattern.
Birr.

177. *Richard Shops, 1970s:*
Blue cotton printed with white and turquoise daisies.
Birr.

178. *Patricia Gray, 1970s:*
Green yellow, pink, orange blue and purple with large floral print.
Birr.

179. *Laura Ashley, 1970s:*
Box dresses.
Birr.

Daywear: Suits

180. *1938:*
Jacket and skirt of blue linen, cream-coloured piping.
Brighton.

181. *1938:*
Jacket and skirt of white linen.
Brighton.

182. *S&M Jacobs, 1950s:*
Coat and skirt made from red petticoat Irish material.
Birr.

183. *S&M Jacobs, 1950s:*
Jacket and skirt of green tweed.
Birr.

184. *S&M Jacobs, 1950s:*
Jacket and skirt of brown tweed.
Birr.

185. *Irene Gilbert, 1950s:*
Green tweed coat and jacket, green patterned silk shirt.
Birr.

186. *Irene Gilbert, 1950s:*
coat and dress of mustard coloured tweed, lined in grey-brown watered silk.
Birr.

187. *1960s:*
Cape and dress of bright purple wool, lined in paisley silk.
Birr.

188. *Thomas Wolfangel, mid-to-late 1960s:*
Suit of emerald-green wool trimmed with black frogging.
Birr.

189. *Thomas Wolfangel, mid-to-late 1960s:*
Navy-blue coat with matching print dress.
Birr.

Daywear: blouses

190. *1930s:*
Black and white checked silk blouse.
Brighton.

191. *1930s:*
Blue and white checked silk blouse.
Brighton.

Evening Dresses

192. *c.1924–25:*
Gold tissue on dark red silk, gilt lace
with diamanté studs.
Brighton, CT004014.

193. *Norman Hartnell, 1929:*
Dark red silk chiffon.
Brighton, CT004010.

194. *Victoire, early 1930s:*
Red silk and silver sequins.
Birr.

195. *Peter Russell, 1933:*
Dress and cape of pink silk.
Brighton.

196. *'Sari' dress, Schiaparelli, 1935:*
White crêpe with blue panels.
Birr.

197. *Schiaparelli, 1935:*
White crêpe.
Birr.

198. *'Beetle' dress, Charles James, 1930s:*
Black and pink metallic thread.
Birr.

199. *Charles James, 1936:*
Pink, blue and amber silk satin with
matching stole.
Brighton, CT004009

200. *'Coq noir' dress, Charles James, c.1937:*
Black faille.
Birr.

201. *'Corselette' or 'la Sylphide' dress, Charles James, c.1937–38:*
White organza over taffeta, white satin,
pink cord.
Birr.
Worn by Susan Armstrong-Jones in
1947.

202. *Molyneux, 1937:*
Black silk chiffon.
Brighton, CT004031.

203. *Charles James, 1938:*
Cream-coloured silk satin and black
Chantilly lace.
Brighton, CT004008.

204. *'Ribbon' ball gown, Charles James, 1939:*
Pink silk faille and organza with
ribbons of various colours.
Worn by Susan Armstrong-Jones in
1947.
Birr.

205. *Jacqmar, 1941:*
Green chenille with purple-coloured glass beading.
Birr.

206. *Irene Gilbert, 1948:*
Scarlet taffeta.
Birr.

207. *John Cavanagh, 1953:*
Cream-coloured and gold silk brocade, fabric designed by Oliver Messel for Sekers.
Brighton, CT004040.

208. *Cocktail outfit, Irene Gilbert, 1950s:*
Olive-green satin coat and green patterned silk dress.
Birr.

209. *Irene Gilbert, early-to-mid 1950s:*
Gold and brown brocade.
Birr.

210. *Irene Gilbert, 1950s:*
Printed brown silk.
Birr.

211. *Irene Gilbert, 1950s:*
Black lace.
Birr.

212. *Irene Gilbert, 1955:*
Pink and purple floral ribbed silk taffeta, with matching shoes, appendix 209.
Brighton, CT004006.1.

213. *Shoes, Holmes, 1955:*
Pink and purple floral ribbed silk taffeta.
Brighton, CT004006.2.

214. *Sybil Connolly, c.1956–58:*
Light brown fabric.
Birr.

215. *Irene Gilbert, late 1950s:*
Black silk with blue daisies.
Birr.

216. *Irene Gilbert, late 1950s:*
Striped black satin and velvet with matching bolero jacket.
Birr.

217. *Irene Gilbert, c.1960:*
White silk embroidered with deep pink carnations.
Brighton.

218. *Cocktail outfit Irene Gilbert, early 1960s:*
Dress: purple satin covered in black net
Coat: purple satin double-breasted swing coat
Hat: purple and black net.
Birr.

219. *'Mermaid' dress, Sybil Connolly, 1960:*
Cream-coloured and gold lace, with matching nylon crepe jacket.
Birr.

220. *Thomas Wolfgangel, mid-to-late 1960s:*
Cream-coloured and purple satin.
Birr

221. *Thomas Wolfgangel, mid-to-late 1960s:*
Red, green and black printed silk.
Birr.

222. *Irene Gilbert, late 1960s:*
Lime green satin with white flowers.
Birr.

223. *Irene Gilbert, 1969:*
Black and cream-coloured silk.
Birr.

224. *Irene Gilbert, 1969:*
Beige silk with matching coat.
Birr.

225. *1960s:*
Green, brown and orange print synthetic material, with gold braid and plastic amber beads. Altered by Anne Rosse.
Birr.

226. *Made by Anne Rosse, 1960s:*
Yellow and black checked cotton, Birr.

227. *1960s–70s:*
Purple, pink, yellow and mauve, swirling floral print, with purple velvet, added by Anne Rosse.
Birr.

228. *1960s–70s:*
Gold brocaded satin with multi-coloured butterflies.
Birr.

229. *1960s–70s, made by Anne Rosse:*
Dress and waistcoat of pink Indian silk embroidered with gold flowers and trimmed with gold-coloured metal discs, made from an old tablecloth.
Birr.

230. *Cocktail outfit, Ib Jorgenson, late 1960s:*
Dress and coat of green silk organza, with beads.
Birr.

231. *Ib Jorgenson, 1970s:*
Black silk crêpe.
Birr.

Outerwear

232. *Chinese ceremonial vest, probably eighteenth century:*
Dark blue embroidered mesh with tasselled fringe, embroidered panel front and back.
Brighton.

233. *Cape, 1930s:*
Black velvet.
Brighton.

234. *Cape, said to have been made by Anne Rosse, 1930s:*
Orange wool.
Birr.

235. *Evening Cloak, c.1935:*
Purple velveteen lined with grey moiré silk with gilt thread tassel and pearls, Brighton, CT004045.

236. *Evening Cloak, mid-1930s:*
Black silk velvet with gold collar.
Birr.

237. *Evening Cloak, mid-1930s:*
Purple velvet, silver collar, with matching bag, appendix 271.
Birr.

238. *Evening Cloak mid-1930s:*
Mauve velvet.
Birr.

239. *'Spider wrap', Charles 1937:*
Black transparent synthetic material.
Brighton.

240. *Evening coat, Charles James, 1938:*
Black velvet.
Brighton, CT004007.

241. *Evening coat, Thomas Wolfangel, mid-to-late 1960s:*
Black gold and cream-coloured print.
Birr.

242. *Evening coat, Thomas Wolfangel, mid-to-late 1960s:*
Black velvet trimmed with frogging.
Birr.

243. *Coat, Thomas Wolfangel, mid-to-late 1960s:*
Blue wool.
Birr.

Special Occasion Clothing

244. *Court feathers and veil, 1922:*
Three white ostrich plumes and tulle veil.
Worn at her presentation at Court in 1922 and 1925.

245. *Wedding Outfit, 1925*
Dress, under dress and train: Ivory satin with pearls.
Shoes, Edward Gerrett & Co: Ivory satin, kid leather lining.
Bag, made by Annie L. Wallace: Ivory satin, trimmed with brown cord, glass beads and sequins, contains an embroidered handkerchief and two notes handwritten by Annie L. Wallace.
Brighton, CT004367.
Worn by Anne at her wedding to

Ronald Owen Lloyd Armstrong-Jones 1925.

246. *Wedding dress, 1935:*
Pale blue silk crêpe.
Birr.
Worn by Anne at her wedding to Michael, 6th Earl of Rosse 1935.

247. *Purse, Duvelleroy, 1935:*
Velvet embroidered in blue, pink, mauve and gilt thread.
Worn by Anne at her wedding to Michael, 6th Earl of Rosse.
Birr.

248. *Wedding trousseau, 1935*
Peach silk nightgown, slip, French knickers and stockings embroidered 'Anne'.
Birr.

249. *Suit, Victor Stiebel, 1960:*
Coat and dress of oyster brocade in moiré pattern.
Birr.
Worn to her son Antony Armstrong-Jones's wedding to Princess Margaret, 1960.

250. *Hat, Simone Mirman, 1960:*
Black and white net.
Birr.
Worn to her son Antony Armstrong-Jones's wedding to Princess Margaret 1960.

Fancy dress

251. *Late 1920s to early 1930s, homemade probably made by Anne, Armstrong-Jones or Oliver Messel:*
Silver and metallic blue gilt thread.
Birr.

252. *Eighteenth-century-style wig, late 1920s to early 1930s, probably made by Oliver Messel.*
Birr.

253. *Kaftans*
Three green/blue with fur.
Birr.

254. *Box labelled fancy dress:*
Various costumes including Victoire dress, bodice with applied 'angel wings', reproduction in calico of Charles James Corselette, and part of Perdita Robinson costume worn in 1928.

255. *Eighteenth-century-style chintz dress.*

Accessories: Furs

256. *Coat, c.1930s:*
Brown ermine.
Brighton.

257. *Stole, c.1930s:*
Sable
Brighton.

258. *Muff, c.1930s:*
Black fur
Brighton.

259. *Hayhill, Jacket, Collar and Hat, c.1930s:*
Black sealskin.
Brighton.

260. *Driving gloves, c. 1930s:*
Brown fur.

Hats

261. *Aage Thaarup, mid 1930s:*
Black trimmed with osprey feathers and heavy net veil.
Brighton.

262. *c.1950s:*
Straw with floral band.
Brighton.

263. *Jacol, c.1950s–6Os:*
Black imitation fur, labelled 'Alice wig'.
Brighton.

264. *Boxes of various hats.*
Birr.

Shoes

265. *Peter Yapp, c.1920s:*
Brown leather brogues, with tassels.
Birr.

266. *Clarks, late 1950s:*
Green suede.
Birr.

267. *Miss Holmes, late 1950s:*
Green patent leather with grosgrain bow.
Birr.

268 *Sandals, late 1950s:*
Cream-coloured fabric, made in Italy.
Birr.

269. *Cameo Room, late 1950s:*
Mauve leather with buckle.
Birr.

270. *Dolcis, late 1950s:*
Pink satin sling back.
Birr.

271. *Dolcis, late 1950s:*
White satin sling back with diamante bow.
Birr.

272. *Dolcis, late 1950s:*
Gold leather.
Birr.

273. *Dolcis, late 1950s:*
Metallic blue-grey satin with silver flower-shaped buckle.
Birr.

274. *Dolcis, late 1950s:*
Bright pink leather shoe with pink grosgrain and black sequin bow.
Birr.

275. *Late 1950s:*
Green satin and velvet.
Birr.

276. *Bag, mid-1930s:*
Purple velvet embroidered in silver threads 'Anne'. Matches appendix 233.
Birr.

277. *Shawl, late 1920s to early 1930s:*
Pale pink printed with flowers in green and blue.
Brighton.

Fifth Generation:
Susan, Viscountess de Vesci (née Armstrong-Jones)

Evening dresses

278. *Sybil Connolly, mid-1950s:*
White draped fabric.
Birr.

279. *Made by Anne Rosse, 1953:*
Yellow silk taffeta with pinky red fabric camellia.

See also appendix 191 & 200

Special Occasion Clothing

280. *Wedding Outfit, 1950*
Dress made by Anne Rosse: Skirt, bodice, underskirt of white silk.
Wedding Shoes: White silk.
Wedding Coronet made by Oliver Messel.
Worn at her wedding to John, 6th Viscount de Vesci, 1950.
Birr.

See also 183–85 & 171

Fifth Generation:
Alison, Countess of Rosse (née Hurle Cooke)

Evening dress

281. *Mary O'Donnell, late 1960s:*
White crochet mini coat-dress.
Birr.

Special Occasion wear

282. *Going-away outfit, 1966:*
Red wool dress and jacket.
Worn after her wedding to William, 7th Earl of Rosse, 1969.

Sixth Generation:
Anna, Lady Oxmantown (née Lin)

Special Occasion wear

283. *Wedding dress, Guyu, designed by Anna Lin, 2004:*
Red embroidered silk.
Birr.
Worn at her wedding to Patrick, Lord Oxmantown, 2004.

284. *Blessing dress, designed by Anna Lin, 2004:*
Cream-coloured embroidered satin with pearls.
Birr.
Worn at the blessing of her marriage to Patrick, Lord Oxmantown, 2004.

Bibliography

The Messel Family, Collections, Houses and Gardens

Armstrong-Jones, Antony, Earl of Snowdon, *A Personal View,* Weidenfeld & Nicolson, London, in Association with Conde Nast, 1979.

Bodkin, Thomas *Hugh Lane and His Pictures,* Pegasus press for the Irish free State Press, 1932.

Castle, Charles, *Oliver Messel: A Biography,* Thames & Hudson, London, 1986.

Deery, Oisin, *A Compact History of Birr,* Tama Books, Dublin, 2001.

Nicholson, Shirley, *Nymans: the story of a Sussex garden,* Sutton in association with the National Trust, Gloucestershire, 1992, 2001.

Nicholson, Shirley, *A Victorian Household,* Sutton Publishing, Gloucestershire, 1994.

Nicholson, Shirley, *An Edwardian Bachelor: Roy Sambourne 1878–1946,* The Victorian Society, 1999.

O'Byrne, Robert, 'Couture for a Countess: Lady Rosse's Wardrobe' *Irish Arts Review Yearbook,* 1996, volume 12, pp157–163.

Pinkham, Roger (ed.), *Oliver Messel,* Victoria & Albert Museum exhibition catalogue, London, 1983.

Taylor, Lou, 'The Wardrobe of Mrs Leonard Messel' *The Englishness of English Dress* Berg, Oxford, 2002.

Fashion/Dress

Blum, Dilys, *Shocking: the Art and Craft of Elsa Schiaparelli,* Philadelphia Museum of Art, USA, 2004.

Brighton Museum & Art Gallery, *Norman Hartnell 1901–1979,* The Royal Pavilion, Art Gallery and Museums, Brighton, 1985.

Coleman, Elizabeth Anne, *The Genius of Charles James,* The Brooklyn Museum, New York, 1982.

de la Haye, Amy (ed.), *The Cutting Edge: Fifty Years of British Fashion 1947–1997,* V&A Publications, London, 1997.

de la Haye, Amy, 'Gilded Brocade Gowns and Impeccable Tailored Tweeds: Victor Stiebel (1907–76) a Quintessentially English Designer' *The Englishness of English Dress* Berg, Oxford, 2002.

Duff Gordon, Lady, *Discretions & Indiscretions,* Jarolds, London, 1932. (This is the autobiography of Lucile).

Hartnell, Norman, *Silver and Gold,* Evans Brothers, London, 1955.

Kjellberg, Anne and North, Susan, *Style & Splendour: the wardrobe of Queen Maud of Norway,* V&A Publications, London, 2005.

McCrum, Elizabeth, *Fabric and Form: Irish fashion since 1950,* Sutton Publishing with Ulster Museum, Belfast, 1997.

Ritblat, Jill, *One Woman's Wardrobe,* Jill Ritblat/Art Data, London, 1998.

Rothstein, Nathalie (ed.), *Four Hundred Years of Fashion,* Victoria & Albert Museum, London, 1992 , re-printed 1996.

Souvenirs Moscovites 1860–1930, Musée Galliera – Musée de la Mode de la Ville de Paris, Paris Musées, 1999. from Guillaume Valérie, Répertoire des Maisons de Couture Russes à Paris.

Vassiliev, Alexandre, *Beauty in Exile,* Harry N Abrams, New York, 1998.

Museology/Interpretation

Belk, Russell, W., *Collecting in a Consumer Society,* Routledge, London, 1995.

Elsner, John and Cardinal, Roger (eds.), *The Cultures of Collecting,* Melbourne University Press, Australia, 1994.

Felshin, Nina, *Empty Dress: clothing as surrogate in recent art,* Independent Curators Incorporated, New York, 1994.

Kavanagh, Gaynor, *Dream Spaces: Memory and the Museum,* Leicester University Press, Leicester, 2000.

Kwint, Marius, Breward, Christopher, Aynsley, Jeremy (eds.), *Material Memories: Design and Evocation,* Berg, Oxford, 1999.

Pearce, Susan M., *Museums, Objects and Collections: A Cultural Study,* Leicester University Press, Leicester, 1993.

Pearce, Susan M., *Interpreting Objects and Collections,* Leicester University Press, Leicester, 1992.

Pearce, Susan M., Collecting in Contemporary Practice, Sage, London, 1997.

Stewart, Susan, *On Longing: Narratives of the Miniature, the Gigantic, the Souvenir, the Collection,* Duke University Press Durham & London, 1993.

Taylor, Lou, *The Study of Dress History,* Manchester University Press, Manchester, 2002.

Taylor, Lou, *Establishing Dress History,* Manchester University Press, Manchester, 2004.

Index

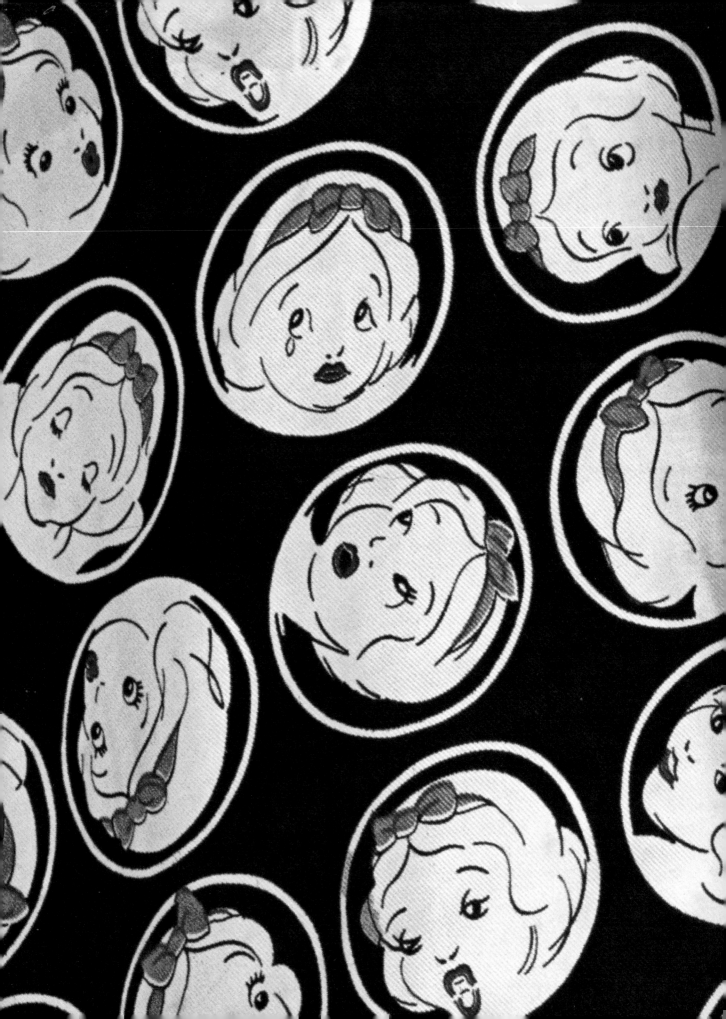